SHRUTI KOHLI is an Indian entrepreneur. She started her career as a journalist and reported for various media organizations, beginning with the central Indian newspaper *The Hitavada*. Subsequently, she reported for *The Times of India*, *The Indian Express*, CNBC TV18, *Outlook Money* and *India Today*. After a decade in journalism, she quit the field in November 2009 to float her own company, Spink Turtle Media Pvt. Ltd, of which she is currently the chairperson and managing director. Her book takes its name from Spink Turtle's magazine for women, *The Petticoat Journal* (www.petticoatjournal.com), which she edits and which is one of the various news, production and event management businesses of her company.

The Petticoat Journal

Money and the Indian Woman

Shruti Kohli

RUPA

Published by
Rupa Publications India Pvt. Ltd 2013
7/16, Ansari Road, Daryaganj
New Delhi 110002

Sales centres:
Allahabad Bengaluru Chennai
Hyderabad Jaipur Kathmandu
Kolkata Mumbai

Copyright © Shruti Kohli 2013

All rights reserved.

No part of this publication may be reproduced, transmitted, or stored in a retrieval system, in any form or by any means, electronic, mechanical, photocopying, recording or otherwise, without the prior permission of the publisher.

ISBN: 978-81-291-2412-8

10 9 8 7 6 5 4 3 2 1

The moral right of the author has been asserted.

Typeset by Jojy Philip, New Delhi.

Printed at Repro Knowledgecast Limited, Thane

This book is sold subject to the condition that it shall not, by way of trade or otherwise, be lent, resold, hired out, or otherwise circulated, without the publisher's prior consent, in any form of binding or cover other than that in which it is published.

To my father, Rajendra Kohli, who smiles at me from heaven whenever I breathe; to my mother, Kiran Kohli, who never lets me waste my time sulking whenever I falter; to my brother, Shashank, who does those little things to make his family feel special; to my teacher, Jenny M. Vyse, who taught me life; to my best friend, Sanjeev, who stood by me through my toughest times; and to you…

Contents

	Introduction	1
1.	The Daughter	9
2.	The Sister	23
3.	The Girlfriend	37
4.	The Bride	51
5.	The Wife	73
6.	The Mother	97
7.	The Mother of a Special Needs Child	122
8.	The Mother-in-Law	133
9.	The Daughter-in-Law	146
10.	The Friend	163
11.	The Single Woman	171
12.	The Professional Woman	184
13.	The Entrepreneur	210
	Parting Words	223
	Acknowledgements	225

Introduction

This is my first book. In that capacity, it should begin right at the beginning. And right in the beginning there is a cheque for Rs 2,000. It's a rainy June afternoon. I take the cheque and walk out of the swanky NIIT office in Jabalpur, my hometown. I pick up my bicycle and start pedalling in the direction of my house. I reach home, hand over the cheque to my parents and go 'Hurrah!' And why not? That, right there, is my life's first paycheque. I am just sixteen years old. And here I am with Rs 2,000 at my disposal every month! It seems like some impossible dream.

I hand over the cheque to my parents and I'm given Rs 2,000 in cash. Out of this, I spend Rs 800 on treating my friends and family to celebrate. Of the rest, I put Rs 100 aside for charity, another Rs 100 goes in my piggy bank, and with the rest I buy canvas, paint and brushes. I am now going to make paintings and greeting cards. During my visit to Delhi earlier that year, a friend had introduced me to a shop that sold handmade cards and paintings by amateur artists. They had offered to exhibit and sell my work.

Two months later, I am ready with three handmade cards and two paintings. I hand these over to the shop on my next visit to Delhi in September that year. A fortnight later, I get a phone call to say that all my stuff has been sold. My profit is a whopping Rs 5,000!

During my research while writing this book, I met a lot of people who questioned my credentials to give advice on money. Some people told me that I had had a well-off upbringing, and so I might not really know about the other side of life, the one without money, this, they thought, made me ineligible to write about the subject.

Well, I wouldn't completely write off their misgivings. I did grow up in affluence: my father was a government servant in the capacity of an engineer. We lived in a sprawling, state-provided bungalow with vast green lawns and two huge kitchen gardens. One of the gardens had a well too! Almost every variety of vegetable and fruit grew in our gardens. The gardens, lawns and other household chores were managed by the state-provided domestic help: Beti bai, Jasodha bai, Pancham bhaiyya, Bihari bhaiyya, Kunjilal bhaiyya, Gopal bhaiyya and Vishnu bhaiyya. My brother and I were undoubtedly born with silver spoons in our mouths.

But consider this: as early adolescents, when my brother and I asked our mother for a new pencil, she would ask us to kneel down at the prayer corner, join our hands, close our eyes, and 'pray to God for a pencil.' We would both obediently follow the instructions. After a while, she would ask us to open our eyes. And bingo, the pencils were right there before us!

It was not just about pencils. Our 'God' gave us anything that we genuinely needed. Yes, mind the word 'genuinely', because our God did not bless us if we lost our things too frequently and came looking for a replacement. He obliged only after we had been punished in school for having lost whatever it was.

This trick was played on us till we were mature enough to understand that it was a trick. But by that time, we had become responsible about our possessions. We had learnt the value of money; we had learnt that it came after much toil.

Besides this, I grew up seeing my father jotting down notes every night in a notebook with a turquoise cover, with inputs from my mother. That was the cash flow record my parents maintained. Ever since I started working, I have also kept a record of my income and daily expenses.

Growing up in such an environment, it's no wonder I did what I did with my first salary!

Actually, my cordial relationship with money has its roots in my father's rags-to-riches story. As a child, my father had seen life without money. This had led him to first pull his parents and siblings out of the debt trap and raise their financial status to a decent level, and then to ensure that his children learnt the value of money from the very beginning. Once my father had finished his engineering studies and found a lucrative government job, the first thing he did was to pay off all his family's debts. Besides this, he handed over his fat salary to his parents every month. With this, the family's financial woes came to an end; none of my father's younger brothers ever had to part with their salaries.

Although my maternal relatives had never seen financially depressed times, my mother always supported my father in his efforts to keep the family finances in perfect order.

When my brother and I started working, each of us had our own struggles with managing our money right. But these were problems common to everyone entering the workforce. I set my house in order a couple of years after I started working. I began by saving, and then moved on to investing. I was to realize the advantage of this later, when I became an entrepreneur and my business went through a difficult patch.

One afternoon in June 2011, I logged on to pay my phone bills. The transaction was unsuccessful! I tried again. Same results! I checked and found, to my shock, that there were only ten rupees in my bank account! The day before, a couple of bills had been paid through ECS and these transactions had slipped my mind. I had never thought it was getting that bad. Since May that year, my business had been registering a slump. And now, my bank balance was zero. Well, almost.

At first, I thought I would have to borrow some money. But then I remembered my investments. I redeemed a couple of mutual fund schemes. However, what with staff salaries, office space rent, and bills to be paid, those saw me through only for two months. Now my net worth was an absolute zero. The returns from my investments and my bank balance had been used up. My rent would be unpaid and my staff would go without salaries for three months.

For a while I thought I had ended up as an also-ran

entrepreneur and that it was time to look for a job. But I was too attached to my baby to abandon it so easily. So I confined myself to the four walls of my flat and worked out a plan to revive my sinking business.

It took me three months to prepare and execute the plan. In the meantime, I picked up an assignment writing weekly columns for a central Indian English daily, *The Hitavada*. This took care of my basic bills for three months. By February 2012, I could see the first ray of hope at the end of the dark, damp tunnel. It came in the form of a sponsorship. We were back in business! There's been no looking back ever since.

Those nine months of financial hardship, from May 2011 to January 2012, was when I applied all the lessons I had learnt from my parents to my own situation. I stayed resolutely away from borrowing. Borrowing was the last of the last options on my list. This again came from my parents, especially my father, who was against borrowing on principle. He even refrained from loans.

The money values my parents inculcated in me have brought me far. They have rescued me from sticky financial situations every now and then. And now I'm writing about these values, so that other people can benefit from them too.

I must move on now to the next question that I have frequently been asked in the course of writing this book. People have asked me: 'Why only for women?'

I decided to specifically address women in this book when I realized that the 'financial independence of women', as we understand it, was a farce! I'll tell you how.

Three years after I started working, I wanted to move to better accommodation, but I realized I could not afford it. This wasn't because I was not earning well. This was because, ever since I began working, I spent as much as I could, or even more than that. I was proud to join the league of 'financially independent' women, which generally meant women who were earning well and could spend at will. But, when my plans to shift to an expensive place faltered, I was forced to question the credibility of this whole notion of 'financial independence'. What to do with the money that you have or earn is almost as difficult a proposition as getting the money!

While reporting a story for CNBC TV18, I met a well-established corporate woman who earned Rs 2.5 lakhs a month. I had gone to interview her for a magazine, and so I asked her about her investments and savings. I mentioned the word 'equities' and I was shocked when she told me that she had no clue what 'equities' meant. It was particularly shocking because she had invested Rs 6 lakhs in stocks.

When I expressed my astonishment, she told me that her husband took care of her salary. She seemed quite happy about the fact. But I wondered if I could truly call her 'financially independent' in my article. She was completely dependent on her husband, who managed her entire salary once it was credited to her account. He mostly invested the money; his idea was that the house would run on his salary and his wife's salary could be used for investments which would also eventually benefit the family. I am not saying that he had mala fide intentions. It is quite natural that when things are going smoothly, nobody thinks about adversity. But I did wonder: what if this woman wanted to buy a diamond pendant? Could she do it from her salary? No, she couldn't! She would have had to ask her husband for it. And God forbid, if she had to walk out on her husband, could she afford to rent her own flat considering the upfront payments involved? No!

Most women in India grow up with the mentality of dependants. They are reared that way, told every now and then, 'You'll be married, after all.' The boyfriend or the husbands bearing the expenses of an outing is regarded as chivalry, even when the woman concerned is earning more than the man. This mindset leads to a situation where the household runs on the husband's salary, and the wife regards her earnings as pocket money.

Then, there are women who are earning good money and have unemployed husbands. They often get beaten up by the men in their lives, and suffer because of that violence, but do not have the guts to walk out. I have come across several cases like this in real life.

Financial independence should render women independent in every way. It's not just about earning a lot of money; it's much more than that. And that is what I have tried to elaborate on in this book.

Women—despite how much we'd like to believe it isn't true—live their lives circumscribed by certain roles that they play in society. A woman is an individual, yes, but she's also a daughter, a mother, a sister, a professional, a daughter-in-law, a girlfriend, a grandmother, and so on. And her monetary worth and her use of her money—whether earned or gifted—inform every one of these relationships. At different stages of our lives, we behave differently. We behave differently in different relationships too. We have to get used to 'his money', 'hers', 'theirs', 'mine', 'ours', and so on. I have thus tried to provide, in this book, viable roadmaps for women in specific roles and relationships.

I have drawn on my own experience, as well as advice and theories from experts in the fields of finance and psychology, in order to draw up these maps. In the chapters that follow, you will get to know a lot about me, my family and friends, my experiences—and I hope you will be able to identify in them circumstances that are familiar to you, and advice that is useful for you.

April 2013   SHRUTI KOHLI
New Delhi

1

The Daughter

Generally speaking, in India, when a daughter is born, she is sometimes made to feel like a liability, while being groomed and prepared to make her a good matrimonial deal. It may look like things are changing among the upper middle class, but that is only a very small section of society. Largely, our society is still not ready to accept a girl. Recent sting operations have exposed female foeticide in rural as well as urban areas, and the sonography and abortion businesses are flourishing, even mushrooming.

Even if a family is not openly vocal about their hatred for a girl, you may notice some troubling undercurrents. People still enthusiastically adhere to age-old traditions which celebrate the birth and life of a male child, but there are no similarly spectacular customs observed to celebrate a girl child. There is a custom among some Hindus where at the age of three, a child's head is shaved clean. Until this ceremony, the child's hair remains uncut; this custom is called mundan. For boys, the mundan is a festive occasion, but for girls, it's a quiet affair; the daughter is just taken to a holy place to have her head shaved.

Similarly, when a boy is born, all the festivals that fall within a year after his birth are celebrated with added pomp. Relatives and friends come bringing presents for the boy on his first Diwali, or his first Lohri. But a girl's first Diwali is celebrated like any other Diwali.

The reason people often give for not wanting a daughter is that 'she will go away one day', while a son will carry the family's name forward, earn and support them. No matter how much you educate your daughter, you are only preparing her for life with another family. I have always wanted to tell these people that their dear son will marry a woman one day. They would (in all probability) like their daughter-in-law to be well-educated and smart, someone who would help their son carry the family's name forward with added glory. So while they are preparing their daughter to live with another family, they are actually preparing for the family that she will be creating and bringing up with her husband. If she does this well, people will praise them for raising such an able woman. And if she does well in her career, people will definitely credit her parents rather than her in-laws.

Among all the various traditions I mentioned above, there is another very significant material tradition attached to daughters. When I was eleven years old, my family and I went on our yearly summer visit to Delhi. As always, the extended family had gathered at my maternal grandparents' house. One evening, we were getting ready to go to my aunt's (my mother's elder sister) house, also in Delhi. When we all sat down to have dinner, I noticed that my maternal grandparents stayed behind in the drawing room. I assumed they must be fasting or something.

But when this happened again, I asked my mother about it. She told me that parents are not supposed to eat or drink at their married daughter's house—according to tradition, since they are not supposed to accept gifts, in cash or kind, from a married daughter.

Later, I found out that this custom has its roots in a historical circumstance. Centuries ago, when daughters were commonly considered property, and were married off with this in mind, it was believed that taking anything material from the married daughter or her in-laws would be tantamount to accepting a price (or bride-price) for her, and would make the marriage look like a monetary transaction. Hence, people would refuse to even eat or drink in their married daughter's new home.

- As a modern woman, you must tell your parents that eating at their married daughter's house, or at a meal hosted by their married daughter or her in-laws, will not disgrace them.

As a teenager, when I understood why my maternal grandparents did not eat or drink at their daughter's house, I wondered, 'What would those parents do who have only female children?' I had seen how my paternal grandparents were financially dependent on my father and their other male children. It was the same with all old couples in those days.

When I was growing up, I was friends with two sisters, who were the daughters of one of my father's colleagues and close friends back in my hometown of Jabalpur. When I found out about the tradition I mentioned above, I thought of them. I thought about these girls' parents. Who would they depend on after their daughters were married off? I never asked anybody, but as I grew up I got my answer.

I have come across a lot of couples who were parents of only daughters. I noticed that most of these parents were financially independent. They had their finances in place so that they did not have to depend on their children in their old age, and they had post-retirement jobs lined up.

Another trend that I have noticed is that if a family owns a business enterprise, the daughters usually join the business after they get married. So even if their parents cannot actively run the business later in their lives, their income will not stop. Basically, the daughter take on the role that a son would usually play. In some cases, even if the family does not have a business, the daughters start one along with their parents, like one of the sisters I mentioned above. Both daughters are married and live in Jabalpur. The younger daughter runs a school from her parents' home; her parents are partners in the business. The other daughter prefers to continue with her job as a web designer with a computer education company in Jabalpur itself.

Mentalities have changed from my grandparents' times to now. Parents are not as fussy about having meals at their married daughters' homes, and they are also opening up to accepting gifts from their daughters' in-laws.

Another family of our family friends in Jabalpur is an old couple. Incidentally, they also have two daughters, both of whom are married; one lives in Jabalpur, and the other in Gurgaon. The parents visit the daughter in Jabalpur quite often and have lunch and dinner at her house. Her in-laws live with her and they are happy to have her parents over for company. They also visit their other daughter in Gurgaon once every three or four months, for a fortnight each time.

It's the same with my cousin's in-laws. They have three daughters. The eldest is married to my cousin and they live in London with their two children. The other two live in the US with their husbands. Their parents visit each daughter once a year, spending at least a month with each of them. And, naturally, they do not stay in hotels when they are visiting them; they stay with their daughters' families.

So, things are changing. But change does not come easy. It tests its makers and beneficiaries before settling in. So, it takes its own time and will not accept you if you do not embrace it. But while some families like the ones I mentioned above have embraced change, some are still struggling to leave old commandments behind. Others are stuck in difficult relationships and are forced to postpone their rendezvous with change.

My friend's neighbour in Mumbai is a sixty-two-year-old woman. She lives alone, and sews clothes for people for a living. Her husband left her enough savings and investments, but these dwindled with time. Thankfully, the flat she lives in is her own. Her married daughter is her only child. She wants to help her mother and look after her, but her husband will not let her do so. He says that if the mother has exhausted all her savings, she can sell off her Bandra West flat, which will fetch her a good price. Why should he deprive his family of a good life by giving money to his mother-in-law?

- Parents will be dependent on their children in their old age, whether they have sons or daughters. This should be made clear to a daughter's prospective husband before marriage.

In this case, the daughter is a housewife, so she is unable to force her husband to help her mother out financially. Much against her husband's wishes, she is now looking for a job. She told him that he would have to agree to her getting a job, or she would walk out. She is facing some difficulties in finding a job, as she has never worked in an office before and she is only a college graduate. But she is determined, and I think she will definitely find a job. I like her concern and determination.

However, she should have made it clear to her husband before they got married that her aging mother had to be looked after. If he was reluctant to devote some part of his salary to this, she should have told him that she would make it work with her own earnings. And if this was also a problem for him, she should have refused to marry him. I know that her mother probably would not have approved of this. But women who have no brothers should not wait for an emergency situation to find employment; they should start working as soon as they finish their education. As the only child of aging parents, your parents should be your topmost priority. They may not let it be known to you that they need financial support from you. But you have to understand that they do.

I would like to mention another possibility here. There have been instances when a prospective groom has agreed to his fiancée's requests before they are married and afterwards gone back on his word. This is unfortunate. Be prepared for such rude shocks and, accordingly, plan for them. If at all possible, you should set things down in writing before marriage, though this would be quite embarrassing and uncomfortable. But it's better to be prepared. If you are working, do not quit your job, no matter what. Your husband may be rich, and he may have agreed to look after your parents. But you do not have to quit working. If you are not working, get a job before you get married.

But just as I was putting this down as a blanket rule, I came across a different scenario. My old flat in Bandra overlooked a home for old women. Sometimes on weekends, when I was home, I saw the inhabitants hanging out on their evening stroll around the grounds of the home. I would invariably curse all the sons who were doing this to their mothers. Then one day my maid told me of a woman who lived a couple of buildings away. This woman was the mother of three daughters, all of whom were married and living in Mumbai. But none could provide shelter and food to their aging mother.

While one of her daughters was a housewife, the other two were working women. However, their excuse was that their salaries sufficed only for their own families and they couldn't afford to look after their mother. Whenever the housewife was asked about her mother, she had just one thing to say: 'She is a strong woman. She can take care of herself. I cannot ask my husband to give her money!' For this category of daughters, my only advice is: get a heart.

These are the people who go to religious places and give away loads of money as charity. But what's the use of such charity when someone in your house or family is struggling to get two meals a day? As a great man said, 'Charity begins at home.' Do it for charity if you have no other emotion for your family. If you have other sisters, do not wait for them to come forward to support your parents. You have to do your bit as much as you can afford. And do not advise your siblings about helping your parents. They may think that you are trying to show off by implying that you care more than they do.

Now, even though I am stressing giving financial support to your aging parents, I must add here that money is not all that matters. Once you have given money to your parents, don't think it's over. They need your company as well. I know an old couple whose daughters live in different cities, while their son lives abroad. The parents have lots of money. Their son, who is a well-off banker, also sends them substantial amounts of money every month. But it makes them sad that their son makes a flying visit for a week each year, and spends only a few hours with them as most of that week is taken up by relatives and friends. So let your money and your emotions both go together. Neither works without either.

Let's look at the other side now. Daughters are sticking to the rulebook. But their parents are so demanding and illogical that nothing seems to make them happy. I'm reminded of a scene from the 2004 sports flick *Million Dollar Baby*.

When the protagonist Maggie, played by Hilary Swank, manages to make enough money by winning boxing championships, she buys a beautiful house for her mother. But when she takes her mother and her sister to see the house, her mother gets upset and says that she should have given her the cash instead, because she needs the money more than she needs a house. Her daughter tells her that she will send her more money. Still the mother is not happy. This obviously leaves the daughter depressed. To this I can't help but say: 'How sharper than a serpent's tooth it is to have a thankless parent.'

A woman once struck up a conversation with me sometime in the year 2005, in a Churchgate-Borivali local train. She was excited about the fact that she had recently learnt how to make cake; she was going to bake one right that evening. Somehow the conversation (which was more of a monologue), shifted to the subject of her twenty-four-year-old daughter. She said that her daughter worked with a BPO and earned a good salary. But she did not know how to contribute towards household expenses. 'She comes back home most evenings carrying vegetables. But she buys them from the most expensive vendor who sits near our building. I have told her many times that she can get them from the wholesale market, but she finds it too much of an effort. On other days she buys stuff like pizza bases and soup powder. My husband and I don't like eating all this. My daughter says she wants us to taste this new-generation food. But it is a waste,' she explained. 'It would be better if she gave some of her salary to us to run the house. We can go out and buy the grocery and vegetables ourselves.'

- You have to handle parents tactfully without hurting their feelings.

Demanding and thankless parents are a reality for some daughters. They can be difficult to placate. Once a woman is married, this stops to some extent. But if she chooses to stay single or is rendered suddenly single, she faces this throughout her life, regardless of her age.

While some mothers adjust like a friend to the lifestyles of their single daughters, others function in constant complaint mode. From 'why do you stay out so late at night?' to 'why do you always come home with those stuffed carry bags?', the questions can be both irritating and guilt-inducing. Of course, we immediately say that parents should change their ways in tune with the changing times. But this is wishful thinking. Although many parents try adjusting, it's often difficult to change one's habits at their age.

- A single daughter living with her mother can be subject to constant comments about her lifestyle. It's difficult to change your parents. It's the daughter who needs to find a way to live her life without feeling guilty about it and without offending her parents.

If your parents don't like certain kinds of food, don't force them to eat it. You wouldn't like it if they forced you to eat karela every day, would you? Secondly, if they want to do the grocery and vegetable shopping, let them do it. They will also object to you spending money on living a good lifestyle. That's because a 'good lifestyle' looks like lavish spending to them. Rather than cribbing or fighting to get your way, have a heart-to-heart with your parents. Tell them you are earning well and are trying to raise your standard of living and that of the family. Tell them that you save enough, even while spending as much as you do. Tell them that these are the returns of all the effort they put in to educate you, and that they must enjoy the returns now without worrying. Don't lose your cool. Your goal is to keep them happy.

Besides this heart-to-heart, involve them in your life by talking to them about your office. Tell them about work and your colleagues, about friends, about that guy who admires you, about anything else that you did during the day. Talk about things that bring happiness, laughter, and smiles to your family. Don't crib about the numerous restrictions they put on you, and don't argue. Fighting with your parents to get your way will get you nowhere, and you will end up feeling guilty. Communication is the key. And remember that you may never be able to completely change their thinking, because they have lived a particular way for a long time, and their social circle also has a similar mindset. If you really want some major changes, it may help to introduce them to men and women of their age group who have a more open outlook on life.

If you are a single woman in your thirties living with your mother, you will have to explain a bit more to her about your financial status. Explain to her that you are earning enough and even when you spend you are being careful about your future and your savings. You may not want to reveal all the details to her, but tell her that you have planned your finances properly, and there is nothing to worry about when you go shopping. An open dialogue like this goes a long way in making things better. Also, try taking her out with you whenever you can. Let her get to know your friends. In brief, treat her as your friend. Introduce her to contemporary books and films that she might enjoy. Your goal is to make her think like your generation, to accept that being single is not a crime or stigma, and that single people are equally competent and smart about organizing their finances.

When you are trying this 'therapy', give your mother or parents at least six months to adapt. It would be unfair to expect them to change immediately. A period of six months will also only show superficial changes. Your parents will be slow to adjust, so don't get worked up too soon. If all these efforts fail—that is, if even after a couple of years, you see no changes in the behaviour of your parent or parents—you will have to shrug off the nagging with a smile each time they come, and carry on with your lifestyle. However, you can still try your best to adjust.

These few instances apart, I feel that, by and large, daughters are quite considerate when it comes to their parents. Frequently, in my experience, they go farther than sons in taking care of their parents. I know of instances when sons have abandoned their parents and a daughter came to their rescue.

At times, sons distance themselves from their parents because of their wives. Women may have problems in adjusting to life with their parents-in-law, and so as daughters-in-law, they may be inconsiderate towards them—this is, unfortunately, a fairly common situation. As daughters, however, they are very thoughtful about their parents' well-being.

THE FILIAL ACCOUNTABILITY THEORY—AND SOME THINGS TO REMEMBER

This theory stresses the daughter's role as a working child of her parents. It calls for the daughter to take on the role conventionally allotted to sons in our society. Daughters who are not working outside the home should also work out strategies with their husbands to support their dependent parents.

- If you can, do contribute towards household expenses as a son would do in a conventional set-up.
- If you are the only child of your parents, you must definitely take responsibility for them.
- Make friends with your nagging mother or father. If

you can accept your friends' weirdness, why not your parents'?
- If you are one of several sisters, and have no brothers, don't wait for your other sisters to support your parents. Support your parents even if you have brothers. Do your bit, and refrain from advising your other siblings about their responsibilities.

2

The Sister

When it comes to money, traditionally, a sister is supposed to be the receiver. She should be showered with gifts, in cash or kind, on occasions or otherwise. Even after she is married, she is supposed to continue to receive gifts, which are now also for her husband and in-laws. This was a tradition because women were not expected to earn, and hence they never assumed the status of earners in a family.

This made the brother, whether younger or older, the decision-making authority in his sister's life. He could stop her from wearing clothes he did not approve of. He could stop her from going out with her friends if he thought it unsafe. Technically, he could control her life. The parents, in most cases, approved of the brother's decisions as he 'had seen the world' thanks to his day-and-night-long outings with his pals.

However, things began to change when women began to enter the workplace. Now, sisters were not ready to obey the restrictions imposed on them by their 'protective' brothers who objected to their clothes and late nights. Even stay-at-home sisters who were not working were influenced by their working counterparts, either through social contact or via the media, and they revolted. But their revolt was short-lived as they were soon married off. Brothers saw this as a direct attack on their authority, which was unacceptable.

Recently, I read a report about a brother killing his sister because she wanted to marry the person she loved and the brother did not approve of her decision. This happened in a state in India where love marriages are condemned, and falling in love is seen as a crime. But the point is that it was the 'protector' brother who killed the sister for overstepping the bounds set by society and her family.

For working women, if they outstay their welcome at their parents' home, which is also shared by their brother(s), there will be discord in the house. Either they get married at the conventional age, or they move out to their own homes if they plan to marry later.

Before we proceed, I must also touch upon the relationship between sisters. To begin with, a woman's relationship with her sister is easy, because as women, they are mostly on the same wavelength. There may be exceptions due to jealousy or sibling rivalry, but sister-sister relations are hardly ever marred by monetary issues.

As I said elsewhere in this book, women in this country often have the misfortune of being abused and disrespected.

A woman may find it hard to protest and difficult to walk out on her brothers who beat her black-and-blue, even if she is the sole breadwinner, and supporting her siblings on her earnings.

Brothers who are unemployed and living on their sisters' money find it hard to accept the fact and look upon it as a disgrace. In our society, an adolescent boy will also behave as the 'man of the family', in which capacity he sees himself as the provider, second only to his father. So it frustrates him to be dependent on his sister's salary, and he takes it out on her. Even younger brothers who are struggling professionally resort to this unbecoming behaviour.

As a sister, you have to work out a strategy to tackle your siblings when it comes to money. Here are some real-life stories of sisters who ended up in adverse situations with their siblings. We'll see what they did, and why and how that can be avoided.

THE OLDER SISTER

As an older sister, if you are in the early stages of your professional life, you can take the liberty to spoil your younger siblings a little. Of course, you have to the draw lines as well. If you are earning well, you can certainly afford to indulge your siblings. But make sure you do not spoil them. Having just started earning, you may be excited about your new financial liberty, and you may want to share the excitement with your brothers and sisters. But be careful that your generosity does not undo the lessons on the value of money that your parents have so painfully taught them.

Apart from this, you have to start organizing your finances. Splurging on your siblings should not derail this. Besides, if you are the sole breadwinner of the family, you may have other financial responsibilities as well.

However, whatever the circumstances, do keep giving your younger siblings little presents occasionally, if you can afford it. I have a couple of friends who have older sisters, and I have heard them complain that their older sisters are just not considerate about giving them gifts, while other people keep boasting about expensive gifts from their older, already-working siblings. At times, your younger brother and sisters may take this to heart and you may end up feeling guilty. However, if you cannot afford it, then I suggest that it's better to live with their resentment and your guilt, rather than ruin your finances.

- If the older earning sister cannot afford to give away expensive gifts to her siblings, she can make smaller contributions.

I know of an older sister who never earned very well. The salary she got was just enough to live on in a metropolitan city. She came from Chandigarh and lived in Mumbai. She had a younger brother, for whom she would always buy small gifts whenever she went home for a visit. But he would always have stories about his friends' older siblings giving them mobile phones or expensive sports shoes. Whatever she did, she would never have the money to match her brother's expectations. As if this guilt was not enough, her brother's close friends and their siblings started giving her brother expensive gifts when they started working. She often felt sorry that she could not afford things like that, but she continued giving him whatever she could manage.

When he grew up and started earning, he stopped telling his sister in as many words that his friends were better than her because they had given him so many expensive presents. But in a moment of disagreement, it all came out. She still feels guilty that as an older sister she could not make her younger brother happy. I tell her that it's not her fault. Her job never paid her enough, and she herself lived on clothes bought from the flea market and had only a very cheap basic mobile phone for a long time. Sadly, such situations and feelings must be endured.

Don't go out of your way. If you cannot afford it, you must not stretch yourself to give gifts or pocket money to your adolescent siblings, just to assuage your feeling of guilt and their feeling of rejection. These feelings will disappear as time passes and people grow up. Someday they will understand your situation. But if your financial foundation becomes shaky early in your life, it can never be mended. At that point, you cannot go to your siblings asking them for money. It will be awkward, and there's no guarantee that they will be in a position to help. What if they are still struggling in their lives, or what if they refuse to help?

- If the older sister's pay does not allow her to set aside money to buy gifts for her siblings, it's better that she live with the guilt rather than stretch her budget beyond her means.

The future is always hazy. You have to stay ready and armed to take on whatever vicissitudes it may have in store for you. Your elders' and other people's experiences will come in handy here. You can observe people who live their life like you do, see what they did or failed to do to tackle adverse situations, and learn from their experiences.

THE SINGLE SISTER

If you are the older unmarried sister of a thirty-something brother who is still professionally struggling, help him out for a while. But if he refuses to work towards improving his situation, you cannot support him for life. You will have to back out. It's not because you cannot afford it. It's because God only helps those who help themselves. If your siblings refuse to get up and sweat for themselves, you cannot do it for them. If you are slogging it out to earn a living, why can't your siblings do the same? We all have to work towards building our own future. Those who think they can do without it just because they have a rich sibling are mistaken.

Now this logic applies for sisters too. If you have a brother who is well-off, you may be all set to take life for granted. Change your ways now, or you will forever live with insult and embarrassment.

Talking of single sisters, if you have lost your job and cannot afford to keep up your lifestyle with your savings, it would be better to curb your expenses and sober up, rather than move in with your brother. In another chapter on single women, I have talked about a real-life instance of a well-established professional woman who left her job in a huff and turned up at her brother's place. The following months were full of physical and verbal violence and agony for the family.

I have come across a lot of instances where brothers are plainly jealous of their 'settled' older sisters. I have been witness to a family fight where the brother, while fighting with his well-established older sister, mockingly says, 'She is a big shot. She is the...what? Yeah, the MD, the *Managing Director,* of a company. She owns a company! Why would she bother about what I or her mother have to say about her language, her dress sense, or her life? She is an independent woman!'

What's worrying is that once men form an opinion, especially a negative one, about the women in their lives, it is hard to change. Even after the brother in the above instance was doing better professionally, his conversation still had an undertone of jealousy in it.

- If you are single, by choice or by chance, and earning well, it is advisable to set your finances in order and refrain from disturbing them, even if your struggling sibling tends to lean on you frequently.
- If you are out of work, it's better to switch to austerity mode and stick around until you get a good job, rather than move to your parents' house, which is shared by your brother.

THE DEPENDENT SISTER

A few years ago, I lived next door to a family which had three children. Their father had retired from an influential corporate position. The oldest child, who was a girl, had married someone who was not ambitious at all. It was 'blind' teenage love that did her in. She was a bright home science student, who had a flair for designing. She created salads and dressings and puddings with amazing finesse. She designed new recipes. She had all the potential to make it big in her field. But then she was introduced to the person she later married, by one of her best friends. He was not even enrolled in a college, and instead, would spend his time hanging out outside the elite girls' college that my neighbour went to. Well, it paid off. For him. He managed to hook this intelligent and promising woman. Much against the will of her family, she eloped with him at the age of twenty one. It's now been about twenty years, and her husband runs an STD and photocopy booth in partnership with his brothers.

The second child, who is a man, is an established professional abroad. The third child is also a woman. The brother has spent lakhs of rupees on 'establishing' his younger sister but she is yet to find her feet. After incurring huge losses in a business that she dabbled in (with her brother's money) for about eight years, she has now got a job. As for the older married sister, despite a jobless and aimless husband, they have their own house, a new car, all the latest gadgets; a luxurious lifestyle, in short. All thanks to her rich brother.

Their brother does all this without his wife's knowledge. He says he does not want unnecessary chaos in his own house. She may have objected early on, when he might have sent some money to his sisters, so he probably stopped telling her about it.

- If sisters continue to live off their brothers after crossing the conventional age of independence, it may lead to embarrassment and insult.

I'm sure a lot of sisters would say, 'What's wrong with this arrangement? Brothers and sisters help each other out financially, if need be.' Well, yes, these sisters may be right. But, if the situation is considered practically, they are in the wrong. It doesn't work like that, you see. There is a lot of unpleasantness involved. Once you cross a certain age, borrowing money from your siblings is like borrowing from another household.

Borrowed money is fun, no doubt, but it brings with it loads of social embarrassment and risk. I say 'risk' because, for instance, in the example above, there is a distinct possibility of upsetting the brother's family. If you think no one will find out about it, you are mistaken. Since the brother has money to spare (he is really very well-established), there is no fear of any upheaval. But if his family suddenly has a need for extra money, his sisters will be left in the lurch, and if he objects to his wife using the surplus income, it may endanger his marriage. Take my word for it, no matter how rich your sibling may be, it's humiliating and risky to live on their money.

If you have a rich married sister, it is even riskier. Although husbands can still function without letting their wives in on their financial dealings, a wife's finances are hardly ever hidden from her husband. Even if the wife is earning her own money, her finances are open to her husband, even though the reverse may not be true. So if you ask your sister for money, you will be putting her in a tough spot.

THE RICH MARRIED SISTER

If you are well-settled, and married to an established, well-off man, while your siblings, older or younger, are not at all financially stable, you may help them financially once in a while, if you are also working and earning well. But again, no matter how well you are earning, you cannot adopt your siblings. You have a lifestyle to match your pay packet, you have necessary expenses relating to your own family lined up, like your children's education, and your own needs. You cannot just let all the burdern of all your family's expenses fall onto your husband and use your salary to support your siblings who refuse to do anything to fix their lives.

- As the working wife of a rich husband, you may help your siblings out once in a while. But you can't adopt them.

If you are a housewife, your siblings should not even look to you for financial help. Your husband may be very well-off, but there are bound to be problems if you use his money for the upkeep of your siblings. It is fine if you have to help them once or twice, but a constant outflow of money from the joint account that you have with your husband to your siblings' accounts can only be the beginning of trouble. It may even lead to the end of your marriage. So when it comes to helping your siblings, show them how to work hard and make money, rather than coddling them. If they do not show enthusiasm in getting up and slogging, it's best to leave them to their fate.

- As the non-working wife of a rich husband, you have to be firm in refusing to extend monetary help to siblings who are able to fend for themselves. If you do not, it will lead to trouble in your family.

There may be parental pressure on you to help your siblings, especially your younger siblings. Parents, particularly mothers, look at things emotionally. They rarely notice that their children are not making enough effort; they see only their failure or bad luck. So they may come to you with requests to help your siblings. But you will have to be emphatic and tell them that they must teach their children to work for themselves rather than live on charity.

- No amount of parental pressure should persuade you to support a sibling who refuses to try to improve their situation.

THE LUCKY NON-ACHIEVERS

I have also seen that if parents are unable to persuade their established children to help their 'struggling' siblings, they will give all their wealth and property to the children who could not achieve anything all through their lives 'despite their sincere efforts'. Their other children, who have slogged all their lives, get peanuts. The argument is that they have enough already and are financially strong, so they obviously have no need of inherited wealth.

Also, these 'hard-working non-achievers' are callous enough to ignore their siblings and grab everything that comes their way. This is one of the reasons for fights over wills.

I know of a family of four sisters and three brothers. The two older brothers and their children are financially well-established. The four sisters are married, and all of them, as well as their children, are well-off. However, one of the sisters is a widow, and while her two children work at multinational companies, they are still not as rich as their cousins. The youngest brother among the seven siblings never really seemed to have much potential. He worked with a company for a while and then set up a small shop which did not do too well. As far as we know, he never tried very hard to get a good job. His mother had a soft corner for him and his two children, and willed all her property to them. All his siblings went along with this because they did not want to fight. Later, all the mother's jewellery also went to this younger brother's wife. The other siblings got nothing at all.

The widowed sister was royally ignored by her own mother and brother, and also by her in-laws. Although her mother-in-law and father-in-law are no longer alive, her youngest brother-in-law, who lives in the family's ancestral home, is eyeing the whole property and trying to have it registered in his name. The widowed sister owns another house, which her husband left to her. While all her brothers-in-law own their own homes, her husband's sisters are not very well-off, but they are not expected to get anything from the ancestral property either.

The point I am making here is that, as a sister, do not expect that you will get the royal treatment from your brothers all your life. Make sure you are financially independent.

- Although the law requires parents to divide their wealth and property equally among all their children, including their daughters, expect your non-achiever brother to walk away with the lion's share even if you are worse-off than him.

THE SPATIAL DEFINITIVENESS THEORY—AND SOME THINGS TO REMEMBER

Siblings are linked by an eternal bond. It's a complicated relationship where, even as they love each other, they may easily come to hate each other; at times, this hatred is irreversible and tends to attain unpleasant proportions. The reason for these relationships going awry is usually money. Earlier, such rivalry and its consequences were mostly between brothers. But now that sisters are also earning and are financially independent, they are a part of this. As the observation goes, women are professionally more sincere, competitive, and consistent. Since they are also emotionally stronger than men, they must actively and intelligently try to keep rivalry out of their relationship with their siblings, even as the sisters stand out as independent entities. They have to define the spaces and boundaries between them and their siblings to maintain a strong bond with them.

- Be supportive, but do not let younger siblings become dependent on you.
- When your younger siblings reach the age where they should be earning, it's best to stop supporting them financially.
- If you have a thirty-something sibling who just doesn't want to work towards financial independence, you need to stop providing for him or her.
- If you are a single woman and are out of a job, resort to austerity till you find another job, rather than falling back on your siblings for monetary help. Don't move in with your parents if a struggling sibling still shares their home.
- If you are a married housewife, it's impossible to go on financially supporting your siblings, unless it is a really dire situation where no one else can help.
- If you are a married working woman, you may want to give some money to your siblings. But do it only if it is really required, such as if a sibling needs help to fund his or her education, and your parents are not around or did not leave enough to help him or her through.
- Rather than supporting them with money, show your struggling siblings the right way to stand on their own two feet.

3

The Girlfriend

When I started working on this chapter, I initially wondered whether I could stretch it to more than a few hundred words. I had thought that the only subject I could write upon here would be the issue of spending on dates, as girlfriends are notorious for making their boyfriends pay for everything. But as I researched and wrote, the words simply flowed.

Ever since I have known about courtships, there have been jokes about how having a girlfriend means empty pockets for men. I had thought that this was a thing of the past. But then in December 2011, I stumbled upon a newspaper report about a twenty-something son of a banker who stole money from his roommate's wallet to buy his girlfriend an expensive gift. The boyfriend was unemployed; he had come to the city to look for a job, and in the course of this, fallen for this girl, who was a college graduate, but had no intention of working. She was all set to be financially dependent on her boyfriend, and later, on her husband.

Well, yes, that's how it traditionally works in our society. It's not incumbent upon women to work. But, you could argue that many women do work for their living. I have lived in Mumbai for nine years now, and I hardly ever come across housewives or non-working girls among women of my generation. From the previous generation too, many women are involved in some professional activity or the other. In many metros as well, the number of working women is on a rise.

The report that I quoted above may just be a one-off incident. I have also come across a lot of couples where both are earning, and earning well. In such cases there are no disagreements about who spends what. In fact, there is no conversation on this topic. But I have also met some couples where the girlfriend does not want to spend, even though she is earning as well as her boyfriend. Towards the other extreme, I have met several couples where the boyfriend is out of work, and the financial needs of the relationship are met by the girlfriend's salary. Yet another extreme is when the girlfriend is not working, has no intention of ever doing so, and the expenses are obviously taken care of by the boyfriend.

All extremes are dangerous. The third instance, where the girlfriend is unemployed, may work well in our society if there is a strong commitment and the relationship evolves into a marriage. Traditionally, in Indian society, the woman is not expected to work and earn outside the home. But in the first two cases, where the working girlfriend is unwilling to part with her money or the boyfriend is jobless, are risky even when there is commitment. This is because even if such a couple manages to float through courtship and get married, there are bound to be problems later on.

- Risky situations:
    - » When a working girlfriend never wants to open her wallet on a date.
    - » When it's only the working girlfriend who pays, as the boyfriend is unemployed for a long time at a stretch, and refuses to take up jobs that come his way.
    - » When the girlfriend is not working, and all expenses are borne by the boyfriend.

I knew one such couple in Mumbai. The girl lived next door to me. As I became friends with her, I came to know that her boyfriend belonged to a rich family but was out of work. He had no qualms about asking his girlfriend to pay his rent, or buy him a pair of shoes. He had rejected jobs because they did not offer him good pay packages, and others because they didn't suit his 'status'.

However, he had all the time in the world to hang out with his friends throughout the week, and on weekends, party with his girlfriend. All this was funded by his girlfriend. If he had really been serious about getting a job, he would have been seen to be working towards it, and he probably would not have remained unemployed for long. This couple had frequent loud fights where the girlfriend refused to give him money or when she questioned what he needed it for. One day I saw a blue mark on her cheek—the fight had now gotten physical! But the relationship never died. A week later, I met the couple at a common friend's birthday bash, where they were both dancing and making merry.

Whenever I see such blindly-in-love couples, I wonder what leads these women into relationships with men who do not have jobs and show no signs of wanting to find one. People say love is blind; I say, 'These women's consciousness is blind.' These men love being dependent. In such cases, the women are responsible for their own unpleasant situations, since they are old enough to see things as they really are. It's really amazing that they should continue supporting such men at their own expense.

Despite their high qualifications and despite holding responsible positions at work, women often fail to make smart choices in relationships. Despite a strong emotional quotient, they show utter lack of emotional intelligence in these matters. Their judgement is overshadowed by the man's good looks or a wealthy background.

But the child of a rich father may not always end up rich, and good looks are no guarantee of wisdom. So judge a man by his own worth, rather than by what his father created. At times, our society is also responsible for these mismatches. No matter how well a woman is doing in her career or how strong she is financially, she is constantly nagged by family and friends to 'have a man in her life'. This is a universal phenomenon. If a professionally established woman is single, her professional achievements are downright disregarded with statements like 'Career, all right. Get a man now.'

At other times, people will tell you, 'Today you feel it's fine to be without a man. You are perfectly happy today. But later you will realize how important it is for a woman to have a man in her life.' Many women are strong and they turn a deaf ear to all this. They are confident about their lives. But some women take this kind of unsolicited advice very seriously, and go on to make the wrong choices.

- Consider the financial aspect when you are getting into a relationship. Money is important. Don't be an idiot and fall for an unemployed man just because 'he has a heart of gold'. The man who is right for you should have a heart of gold and a head for diamonds.

Let your head rule your heart when it comes to relationships. Leave the mushy duets to the movies. Make it clear to yourself that, no matter what, you will not enter into a relationship with a person who cannot keep his job, who rejects the job offers he gets as 'below his standards', who is not embarrassed to live off your money. Rather than going by his looks and his father's net worth, judge him by his personality and his character. If he develops cold feet when asked to stand on his own, reject him. You cannot afford to be a crutch for a man who is perfectly capable of running; you need to stand up for yourself too.

However, this kind of man is not to be confused with someone who is working hard to achieve a goal and is still struggling. If you were born with a silver spoon in your mouth, while the man you are seeing comes from a humble background but is working hard to make it big, then you must look at this positively. If both of you get on well, and neither of you sees your social background as a hurdle, you are a perfect match. But generally, such a match is a rarity. The person who comes from a higher social stratum is often insecure that their partner is only with them because of their social status. Although they may not openly express this, somewhere deep down they always feel that it's their wealth and not them that attracts their partner. For such women, my advice is that if you are fond of a man from a modest background, who is in the process of achieving his goal, wait till he has reached it.

I must tell you about a couple who parted ways because a rich woman developed a sudden insecurity about her man's intentions.

I was visiting one of my ex-roommates in Mumbai, who had moved out of our flat after she got married. We were talking about relationships and marriages and she told me about one of her friends who was in the process of a break-up with her partner. The friend was from a rich Marwari family, and ran a diamond jewellery business. She was seeing a man who was from a middle-class family, much less well-off. He was a software engineer with a multinational company. One day, my ex-roommate met the couple at a cafe. As soon as the friend's partner came in, he praised the new diamond ring that she was wearing. Afterwards, my roommate told her friend that it seemed that he was only interested in her wealth, since he praised her diamond ring rather than her beauty. Another time, at a party, he praised the Versace dress that his girlfriend was wearing. A few days later, she called up my friend to inform her that she had finally realized that her boyfriend was after her wealth. He was always admiring and praising her dresses and jewellery, and he loved visiting her jewellery outlet.

The more I come across such cases, the more my conviction that this kind of match is always a mismatch is strengthened. A relationship between a man of a higher social status and a woman of a lower social status may still work, as women are socially conditioned to be submissive. But never the other way around. Consequently, a relationship between a man of a lower social status and a woman belonging to a higher social strata rarely works.

Now this should not be confused with a situation where a man who is well-settled wants a working girlfriend or wife. One of my colleagues, at the news channel I worked for, would tell us quite often that if he ever had a girlfriend, she would have to be a working woman, because going to office and working with people opens up a person's mind.

In such a set-up where both partners are working, and are responsible enough, there are bound to be fewer problems. People who think like my colleague are actually recognizing the importance of women's financial independence. Isn't that what women want?

However, that's only if it works out well. There is quite a gap between believing something and implementing it. If your boyfriend is open to the changing scenario, enjoy it; but just to make sure that his attitude does not change, as a girlfriend you must be careful about a couple of things.

To begin with, always be generous when it comes to spending during outings and dates. If your boyfriend is not comfortable with you footing the bill, go Dutch. Sharing the expenses equally will help in the long run. He may want to spend on you out of chivalry. That's great, but when the going gets tough, he may use that against you. 'You had a ball with my money and now you refuse to listen to me!' All will fail, the male ego shall prevail.

- As a girlfriend, always be willing to bear the expenses during dates with your boyfriend.

Remember whenever you are living on someone else's money, whether it be your friend's, your boyfriend's or your husband's, you will have to keep your back bent in front of them, and take criticism without protest. I have heard a lot of girls complaining, 'These guys take us out, spend on us ...they do all of it to sleep with us easily.' I tell these girls, 'Well, then, you take them out, spend on them, and then *you* take a call about who gets laid or not.'

However, while you do your bit to be the financial boss, beware of a guy who starts depending on your money, either because he is jobless and aimless, or because he is saving his salary for some bigger personal goal. I knew a couple in Delhi where all the expenses were taken care of by the girl. She enjoyed being centre stage, which boosted self-respect. But actually, she was being fooled. Her boyfriend was saving his salary to buy a house. When he did finally purchase one, and she expressed her desire for marriage, he refused. The reason that he gave her was even more shocking. He said,

'You are an independent woman. Why would you need to get married? Men should marry women who need them, and not someone who is so financially independent. You will find one thousand ways and means to live.' They broke up.

The lesson here is that don't overdo anything. People say in the context of food, 'An excess of anything is harmful.' This useful rule applies here as well. Don't go overboard trying to establish your self-respect. Set limits and stick to them. The moment you feel an imbalance, it's time to retreat. Tell your partner he must share expenditures. If he is reluctant, you must also refuse to spend anything. And when your boyfriend is also earning well, the only way to go is Dutch.

- It's good that the girlfriend takes charge when it comes to spending. But don't overdo it. Know where to draw the line and when not to cross it.

Some years ago, one of my flatmates, who was doing very well in her career and lived a life to match her salary, was seeing a man who was equally well-settled. On quite a few occasions she would come home with expensive gifts, courtesy her boyfriend. One day she showed me a Tommy Hilfiger watch, which she had bought for her boyfriend. That evening, she explained the arrangement: she was particular about keeping the gifting balanced. In fact, she would try and give him more presents than he gave her, and she also sometimes declined to accept his gifts. This is the perfect arrangement. Such relationships never fall apart; there may be other serious issues, but money will never be the reason for the split.

- If your boyfriend loves showering you with expensive gifts, make sure you start to love showering him with equally or more expensive gifts.

On another note, interestingly, some women are wary of rich men. They are hung up on the belief that money corrupts. Promoted by elders and an endless number of movies, this is embedded in the psyche of our youngsters, especially women. Once I overheard a woman tell another, 'He is rich, but he is a very good man. I have never heard anything negative about him.' Our movies inevitably present you with a villain who is super-rich and a hero who is either poor or not-so-rich, and holds the moral high ground. The reality is that these are bookish and celluloid generalizations. Not all rich men are bad, and neither are all not-so-rich men good. Let's not paint them in black and white. Some are grey as well!

But I do have a word of caution when it comes to rich men. I have heard about a lot of women who come to big cities to make it big in their careers. They end up living a wealthy, posh life not by getting big breaks but by entering into relationships with actors, industrialists and other rich men, who are mostly already married. Barely half a per cent of these women get a career break from this kind of arrangement; a majority of women in such relationships end up emotional wrecks. Also, women in such relationships are not called 'girlfriends'. They are mistresses, let's face it. It's not a very good idea to get into a relationship for money. I may sound harsh, but the status of a woman in this kind of a relationship is worse than that of a slave.

A few years ago, one of my ex-colleague's flatmates, a twenty-something woman, was having an affair with a well-known middle-aged Bollywood actor. Even though she was not employed anywhere, she enjoyed a lavish lifestyle which, in Mumbai, is generally the prerogative of established people and their families. However, as the knowledge of her financial situation spread and people began to whisper about it, she began to distance herself from everyone around her. Eventually, she became completely aloof and disconnected from all her acquaintances.

- Don't strike up relationships with influential men just because you believe that they can help you achieve your ambitions.

It's tough to earn money, especially for women. We still live in a society where the woman is regarded as 'the culprit' in any illegitimate relationship. Sucking up to a rich man because he is rich and he promises to help you get your big break will bring you nothing but momentary happiness and loads of humiliation and anxiety later. Women are gifted with a very strong sense of judgement. We are quick to recognize a person's character. But this will help only if we decide to put our special abilities to use. Only if you think you can handle the aftermath of your relationship ending should you go ahead with it.

All this while we have been discussing how you, as a girlfriend, should handle money. Now let's look at that in-between status when a man shows some interest in you and you go on a date to see if you want to take the acquaintance further. The blanket rule is: you foot the bill. Even if he insists that he will pay, politely refuse. Be careful that this does not turn into an unpleasant argument. If at any point you feel it is becoming too awkward, give in and go Dutch. Now, in this case, if you pay by card and he pays his half to you in cash, don't get fussy about change. For instance, if half the amount of the bill comes to Rs 480 and he gives you Rs 500, don't ransack your wallet to find a Rs 20 note. Let it go. Keep the Rs 500 note. I'm bringing this up because women tend to go overboard for miniscule amounts of money.

- When on a first or second date, which may or may not lead to a relationship, the girl must foot the bill.

Throughout this chapter we have talked about a woman's relationship with a man in the capacity of a girlfriend. But there are also same-sex couples. Here, since both the partners are women, they are usually on a similar wavelength. So it's rare that money is the cause of problems in their relationship. However, during my research for this book, I did bump into a lesbian couple who were facing problems relating to money, mostly about who spent what and how much. In these cases, I would suggest that the couple 'go Dutch'.

As well, if you are in a same-sex relationship and living together like a married couple would, stick to the individual-joint-individual account set up. The couple can have a joint account along with their individual accounts, and each partner can contribute equally towards expenses. If one of the partners insists that she take care of all the household expenses herself, she should realize that this will not work in the long run. Communication will help sort things out.

THE INTEGRATED MINDFULNESS THEORY—AND SOME THINGS TO REMEMBER

This theory is about attachment without clinging. As a girlfriend, you have to establish a connect with your partner without either of you being dependent on the other. As opposed to marriages, relationships are very fragile and complex. There are usually no families involved to provide the intervention and wisdom of older people. So, the wisdom and alertness will have to come from you, the girlfriend, because when things go awry, even in these times, the blame falls on the girl. To top it all, if the male partner was spending more on the relationship all through, you will be in the weaker position. You will have the upper hand if you aggressively manage all your joint expenses.

- Avoid unemployed boyfriends who show no enthusiasm about finding a job anytime soon.
- Foot the bills on dates with your boyfriend. If he insists on paying, go Dutch.
- Say no to 'financially beneficial' relationships with rich men, whether they're married or unmarried, unless you feel confident that you can handle the consequences.

- Even if you're paying by card, make the payment and let your friend make the reimbursement for his share in cash to you.
- If you are going out on a first date, foot the bill, no matter what. If he insists on paying, and you think it may turn into an argument, go Dutch. But under no circumstances should you let him pay the whole amount.
- If both partners in a relationship are women, it's again advisable to go Dutch. If you are living together, both partners should contribute equally towards household expenditures.

4

The Bride

Career and marriage are two of the most important junctures in a person's life. Until recently, for women in India, marriage was the only significant turning point in life. But this was also largely taken care of by one's family and well-wishers. The woman was just required to say 'yes' to her family's choice of groom for her, and then spend the rest of her life 'serving' her husband and her in-laws.

Another important aspect of marriage is dowry. It is still prevalent, in fact the practice is growing by the day. Until recently, a bride could not afford to go against her family, even in something as crucial as marriage. This was because women were financially dependent on their fathers and brothers before marriage. The men of the family were the self-appointed protectors and mentors of women. The women, then, had to live the life chosen for them, and accept traditions like dowry, even if they were against the law.

Now that more women are working and are financially independent, as far as choosing a bridegroom is concerned, something has changed. In many cases, women are making their own choice about a husband. However, nothing has changed as far as illegal archaic traditions like dowry are concerned. For many upper-middle-class, educated families, dowry is a status symbol and among the not-so-rich and the poorer sections of society, it is a customary demand of the groom's family which must be religiously fulfilled by the bride's family if they want to see their daughter married.

GIRLS ARE A BURDEN

Once, on one of my reporting assignments, I went to Udaipur in Rajasthan. This state is notorious for female foeticide and child marriage. I happened to meet a social worker involved with a well-known non-profit organization, Seva Mandir. Although the NGO does not work in this field, I was curious, so I asked this social worker about the high rate of female foeticide and child marriages in Rajasthan. Since he was a local, I felt he would be able to give me the true story. He told me, 'People believe a girl is a burden. From the moment she is born, you have added responsibilities on your shoulders. It means expenses, expenses, and more expenses, and no income from her. You spend on her education, then by the time she is prepared to use that education and earn money, she is supposed to get married and join another family. Throughout your life, you only spend on your daughter. Even after her marriage, you are required to keep showering her and her in-laws with expensive gifts, whether you can afford it or not. And then there's dowry, the fattest of all expenses on a daughter.'

This is not just about one region or state. People across the country have this kind of mentality about girls. Did you just say, 'Dowry is dead in urban areas'? I have attended at least three upper-middle-class weddings over the last year. At each of these marriages, the bride's parents gave gold jewellery, furniture, cars and clothes to the groom's family. It is all easily passed off as a 'gift' they are giving to their daughter.

- Dowry is still largely responsible for people's aversion to having a daughter.

This chapter is for all the women who are about to get married or plan to get married later. They need to know that marriage is a very crucial event in a woman's life. More than a man, it's the woman who starts a new life. She usually moves to a new house. She joins a new family, and needs to adjust to new people on daily basis. She must be more involved in the entire process, beginning from choosing a groom to objecting to unlawful practices like dowry.

Despite stringent laws designed to curb the practice, dowry still exists, in all its glory. Along with others, I hold women, particularly brides, equally responsible for this. They never object to dowry. Some women go about the wedding process like dumb dolls, as if their only involvement is to get decked up and dream about the wedding night. They are not in the least concerned about things like dowry. In some families, where the daughters do object, they are asked not to bother with all this.

- Brides have to come forward to help end the system of dowry and save girls from being hated and unwanted.

I strongly believe that the bride should put her foot down, and tell her parents and her prospective husband that no dowry should be associated with her marriage. If they do not agree, the girl should refuse to marry. We need to resort to such means now, because this social disgrace refuses to fade.

Sometime in 2010, my maid in Mumbai told me that she had wanted to get her daughter married that year, but that she had to wait for another year, as she did not have the money for her dowry. She was also concerned that she had spent a lot on educating her daughter. If she had not spent so much money on her education, she would have enough money for her dowry now. She said that all that education was of no use, as her daughter would end up doing the housework at her husband's home like any other uneducated girl would. I asked her, 'Didn't her education help get a better husband for her, and why is dowry so mandatory?' She looked at me, surprised, and then replied, 'What are you saying? Who will marry our daughters without dowry?' She told me the bridegroom was an auto-rickshaw driver. Her daughter had completed high school, but she decided not to educate her further, because it was too expensive. My maid's husband is a linesman. Both parents together are unable to make enough money to educate both their daughters and then save up for their dowry as well. No wonder there is so much hatred for the girl child and no wonder the tradition of female foeticide still endures.

- The poor struggle to meet dowry demands, even as it becomes a status symbol for the rich.

Even as families with little or no money struggle to meet dowry demands, dowry is a status symbol for affluent families. Flaunting the amount of dowry they give to their daughter when she gets married is a matter of pride. It is a remark on their financial status, so much so, that if the groom's family refuses to accept any dowry, the bride's family takes it as an insult. In one such family that I know in Delhi, the bridegroom knew what was being given to his family as dowry, but his parents had no clue. A day after the wedding, a lorry loaded with expensive stuff rolled into the groom's driveway, followed by a Skoda, which was also a part of the dowry. His parents were shocked. The groom tried to explain, but to no avail. His father immediately called the bride's parents, and told them that he and his family were against dowry, and that he was returning everything. After he had hung up, his brand-new daughter-in-law said angrily, 'You think my parents are poor people and cannot afford all this? How can you return something that my parents have sent as a token of affection at my wedding?' Her husband agreed, and asked his father to keep everything as a gift. His parents refused. The girl packed her bags at once and went to her parents' home. Her husband followed her to bring her back, but she would not go without the dowry.

The matter could not be settled, and the newlyweds shifted to a separate home provided by the bride's parents, along with all the things that had come as dowry. What foolishness by the woman and what bigger foolishness by the man! The husband should have left his wife at her parents' home if she refused to return. It was utter foolishness on his part to have gone along with her in her stupidity. The bride was foolish because despite marrying into a rich family, she acted as she did. The groom worked with a company in Gurgaon and was earning very well. He was an only child, and would eventually inherit everything his parents had. But after this incident, his father left all his property to an orphanage.

The stark similarity between this case and my maid's daughter's case is that in neither case is the bride opposing the practice of dowry. In fact, in the former case, she is openly supporting it. Later, if things don't go according to plan, the bride might use, or rather, misuse the dowry laws. My maid's daughter might be brought back to her parents' home in the auto-rickshaw one fine day. She would accept that as her fate and get on with her life, probably following her mother's profession. But in more affluent families, if the girl returns to her parents' home, and the groom sides with his parents, the girl along with her family would definitely fight for her rights. After all, why not? Women have been subjected to misery for far too long.

In the case above, judging by the aggressiveness displayed by the bride, if the groom had not agreed to move out with her, chances are that the bride and her family would have tortured the groom and his family. The dowry laws in India favour women, which is good, considering that women have borne so many atrocities for so long. But these laws can also be misused by disgruntled daughters-in-law.

- Some women consider it an insult to their parents if their husband and in-laws refuse to take any dowry.

In the course of writing this book, I met a woman whose forty-year-old cousin married a decent, handsome man fifteen years ago. Barely four years after her marriage, she returned home one evening, crying. She had been complaining about her nagging mother-in-law for the last one year. Now, she had come back with her one-year-old son, saying she could not adjust to living with her mother-in-law. Having failed to change her mind, her husband and his family gave in, but asked her to leave the son with them. This made the woman furious, and she slapped a dowry case on her husband, his sister, his younger brother and his mother. The case dragged on for eight years. After a while, the husband and his family approached the woman to settle the case out of court. She agreed, but only in return for a hefty sum of money, and also full custody of her son.

One of my distant cousins recently got married. His family's house was redone a couple of months before the wedding, but my cousin's bedroom was left without furniture until a couple of days before the wedding, when the furniture, 'gifted' by the bride's family, arrived. Along with the bed, there was an LCD TV, a dressing table and three cupboards. A couple of days after the marriage came the drawing room furniture. This was all besides the jewellery and clothes which are now regarded as a tradition.

Another cousin was scheduled to get married about three months later. The mothers of both my cousins had a dowry tête-à-tête. The mother of the cousin who was already married gave her relative details about what they had received, and the other mother gave all the particulars of what was coming to her family, each in a bid to show that they were getting more than the other one.

- Dowry is a status symbol for the upper middle class.

I wonder what would have happened if both these brides had objected to taking dowry along with them. Had the bridegrooms' families insisted on taking dowry? Had they threatened to call off the marriage if the brides did not budge? Even if the marriages had materialized without dowry, would the families of the grooms and the brides have gossiped about the inability of the brides' parents to 'properly' manage their daughters' weddings? Would they have attacked at the brides' parents' social status? Would the brides have been unable to make a respectable place for themselves and their families in their husbands' houses? Would the husbands and their families have harassed the bride throughout their lives? Anything is possible. But all these cases of dowry that we hear about are mostly from the upper middle class. Ironically, these are the families where daughters and brides are well-educated and capable of standing up against what is wrong.

OPPOSE DOWRY, BUT SMARTLY

It's time brides wake up. But you must do it smartly. Don't jump into any course of action unprepared. Get your facts right, and then move ahead intelligently. If you are getting married and have plans to do an anti-dowry crusade, make sure your in-laws and your prospective husband are in line with your ideologies. Also, when you are opposing your parents on dowry issues, there is no need to do a Joan of Arc on them. They are not your enemies, and you are not fighting to free a country from them. Talk to them. I know the first couple of times you may fail in convincing them that they should not waste their time and money on dowry shopping for you. Even if they agree, there will be pressure from relatives who will tell them it is humiliating. So be ready for a series of private conversations with your parents. If you have siblings around your age, start with them. They will definitely support you.

Your mission should be to keep dowry out of your marriage. It will save you from a lot of related trouble.

- If, as a bride, you are all set to oppose dowry in your marriage, do it smartly. Get your parents, prospective groom and his parents on your side. Talk to them. Get your siblings and cousins of your age group to support you.

The tradition of dowry has various explanations. It is given to help the newlywed couple set up their new home. In some cultures, it is given to support the bride and her children if her husband dies. It is also a compensation for the bride-price which is more common in polygamous societies. Dowry is also given to a bride as a form of protection against ill-treatment by in-laws. It serves as a 'bribe' to the groom and his family to refrain from ill-treating the bride.

However, a more relevant explanation for dowry is that it is given to a bride as her personal wealth. Since most women did not work outside the home, dowry served as their personal material assets. To make sure that their daughter is financially secure after marriage, parents load her with dowry at the time of her marriage. But over the years, dowry has attained abominable proportions. This has happened because the groom and his family started seeing a dowry as their right, whereas according to every culture and tradition, it was actually meant for the bride's comfort. It was meant to be a financial security for the bride, rather than her husband or in-laws. However, since more women are working now, and have some personal wealth, dowry is nothing more than a gesture, or a status symbol.

It's because of this hateful compulsion of loading daughters up with valuables when they leave for their husbands' home that makes daughters seem like burdens. They grow up hearing this; if their parents don't say it, their relatives do. If they don't say it with a stern, serious face, they say it with a laugh. If nobody else, movies and soap operas do the trick. Even if a woman is working and absolutely independent, there is always pressure on her to find a man and become dependent ASAP.

Consider this. There is a family of four—a mother, two

daughters and a son. The father passed away a few years ago. All three children, who are now in their late twenties, are working. The women, after returning home from work, help their mother in the kitchen. The son, after returning home, relaxes in front of the TV. On weekends, the daughters help their mother with household tasks. The son watches movies, or simply sleeps, or hangs out with his friends. So, who's the burden now?

Girls were regarded as burdens because in conventional set-ups, they did not add material value to the family in any way. They never went out to work and earn money like their brothers. Helping mothers at home with household work has never counted as adding quality value; most of the time, it's not even recognized as labour. So, even as the sons were left alone to study so that they could be eligible to add financial value to the family's well-being, in many pockets in India, girls were married off as young as seven and eight years old. Education had no meaning in their lives, because an educational qualification is largely seen as only an eligibility criteria for matrimonial alliances.

EDUCATION AS A MATRIMONIAL CRITERION

The daughter of one of our family friends finished her MBA with flying colours last year from a prestigious college in Pune. She had earlier studied engineering. She was offered a good job in Pune, as well as one in Mumbai. But her parents summoned her back home, and they are now looking for a 'suitable boy' for her. She is not working anywhere as of now; her MBA and engineering degrees were meant to get her a good groom and in-laws.

- A girl was regarded as a burden or a liability in her parents' home, as traditionally she did not contribute to the family's income.
- Daughters have started earning now. But the perception is that they will not be able to add monetary value to their parents' account for long, as when they get married, they will move to their husbands' home.

Such a mentality keeps girls and their parents under pressure to find a 'good' match. In many cases, this is why women make wrong choices. They are under such tremendous pressure that they don't mind compromising on several very important counts while choosing a groom. Professionally well-settled women marry jobless or struggling men. They are unable to end the marriage even when they realize they've taken a wrong decision, all because of social pressure. A divorced woman is generally a cause of disgrace for her parents. If she has children, they become her reason for not having the guts to walk out of the marriage. I have come across a lot of women who have spent their lives in unhappy, rough marriages, just because walking out would bring disgrace to them and their families.

HIS FINANCIAL STATUS MATTERS

Another very important aspect that women tend to overlook when getting married is the groom's financial status. Those women who tell me that they will choose a husband only on the basis of his character, and that money does not matter, must know that they are being utterly foolish. He should be a good person, no doubt. But money matters too!

- If 'financial status' is not a criterion for you while choosing a husband, you are doing it wrong!

If you are a working woman and your prospective husband earns less than you, there may be a problem later in life. Most men who earn less than their wives become a bit difficult to handle as they tend to get cranky a few years down the line. When I say 'less', I mean less by forty or fifty per cent. A difference of five or ten per cent between your salaries usually goes unnoticed. If you have known someone for a long time, you would know how he reacts to such a situation. If it's an arranged marriage, make it a point to get to know a person's mindset and his thoughts on husbands earning less than their wives before you say 'yes'.

Most men say they have no problems with their wives earning more than them, but when they are faced with an uncomfortable situation that has arisen because of such a discrepancy, they can react badly. Make them aware of the situation before you get married. You do not have to boast about your fat salary, there are a lot of other ways to do this. Go out with him to gatherings of his friends, and invite him to your friends' parties. Mix with his friends and make sure he opens up to yours. Slowly, you will be able to read him. He must appreciate you for your success, rather than feel bad about being far behind you. As for you, you must not brag about your salary. This is definitely repulsive, and if you do this, sooner or later, he will say 'no'.

- Don't boast about your higher salary and professional status to your prospective husband. This will put him off, even if he is open to the idea of the wife being professionally more successful than her husband.

We should also talk about a situation where you meet a man who is earning much more than you do. Traditionally, this is a perfect match. But some women are too competitive and look at their husbands also as professional competitors. If you are one of them, then it is advisable that you don't agree to such a marriage. Also, I must add here that if you are so competitive, it will be difficult for you to find a match. You will have to find someone who earns less than you do and does not care about these things. He must also be less ambitious than you are, or else he might start earning more than you later on, which is bound to make you uncomfortable, and your marriage might suffer.

LOOKING FOR RICH WIVES

Now I must tell you about a rare but nevertheless existent category of prospective grooms. These are the ones who plan to stay home after getting married, while their wives go to office. These men look for rich, independent women to marry. For instance, among the series of matrimonial suggestions that I have received from my relatives over the last few years, one was an acquaintance of my cousin.

He lived in Canada and worked in a bank. So far, so impressive.

When he called one morning, I kept the first conversation with him very short, only exchanging pleasantries. Over our next three conversations that I had with him, I was in for a shock. He cribbed about his current job and boss for a long time. Then he complained about his previous jobs and bosses. Then he told me that he was fed up of taking nonsense from his bosses. He wanted to be independent. What I understood was that he wanted to start a business. But he had other intentions. He said, 'I am looking for a rich, independent wife. I am fed up of working, and after marriage I intend to stay at home while my wife works. I am ready to do the household chores. I'm ready to do the crap work that women generally do and crib about. As a person, I am very good. So why should it be difficult for women to accept me as their husband?' The first time he said this, I took it as the ranting of a tired mind. But he said the same thing during two consecutive conversations. Well, there was a time when men were wary that women were marrying them for their wealth rather than their personalities. Times have changed. Now women also have to be careful about such things. See? Financial independence comes with some strings attached.

- Some men want to marry a well-established rich woman, and take voluntary retirement after marriage.

On questioning this man a bit, I figured out that his professional graph had been a horizontal line ever since he started his career. He had studied hotel management, but failed to keep the job that he got with a hotel. After working in various sectors, he was now working with a bank and again having problems with his boss. He also cribbed about his salary. It was frustrating for him that at thirty-four, he was still employed at a junior level. It was a low-paid job, no doubt. But who is responsible for it? After eighteen years of age, each one of us is 100 per cent responsible for what we are.

I stopped taking his calls after telling him what was wrong. But I don't think a person like him will ever do anything to change. My advice to all prospective brides: avoid them! They will never add any value to your life, or to your household, for that matter. They are disgusted with their lives, and after marriage they will make you feel disgusted about their lives and the life you share together as well.

If a person is not honest enough to tell you about his humble future plans, you should be able to judge what they might be from their conversation. If you are in a relationship with a person who dreams big but refuses to work hard, do not turn your relationship into a marriage. Women generally put their heart before their head in deciding such matters. But it's time your head got its due space. I have heard girls say, 'How can I leave him? He is such a good guy! And he will find a job sooner or later. No one remains unemployed all through their lives.' Go and see the world, girl! Unemployed husbands are a flourishing species, and they are a pain exactly where it hurts the most.

One of my teachers, who taught me social science in

school, married a man she had met in college. They had dated for five years before they got married. After finishing college, my teacher had found a job at my school. But the man she was seeing chose to remain jobless. His occupation was to get dressed up and hang out with other unemployed men. Still, they got married. It has been seventeen years since their marriage now. They have a teenage daughter who has been led astray. My schoolteacher has paralysis. The story is that her unemployed husband beats her up when he does not get direct access to her wallet. A series of such physical attacks rendered her paralytic. The school is finding it hard to retain her on their payroll, as she is not able to teach any more. However, as per the law, they cannot terminate her services on medical grounds. So, they have slashed her salary from the initial Rs 20,000 to Rs 10,000, which is all that the family has to depend on.

I have asked many women in such situations why they won't just leave. Walk out, and the rest will be taken care of. But, they tell me it's really difficult to gather the guts to 'take such a bold step'. I have discussed this more elaborately in the chapter 'The Wife'. It's social pressure that makes women stay in bad marriages. They take violence and insults from their jobless, alcoholic men, but cannot gather the courage to move out. To a very large extent these women's parents, especially their mothers, are to be blamed. They discourage their daughters from ending the marriage on the premise that 'Women must endure.' This is abhorrent! It's criminal! In some cases I have come across, men threaten their wives if they talk of divorce or separation. In such instances, women have to find a way and opportunity to report the matter to an authority, or talk about it with a close friend or relative who can help them out of the mess.

- Women who are getting beaten up by their husbands must immediately walk out and end the marriage.
- If women are threatened by their husbands or discouraged by their parents when they express their desire to end the marriage, they must find another way of doing it.

WEDDING EXPENSES

Another important financial aspect related to marriage is the wedding expenses. In India, a wedding comprises a series of rituals which can last for four to five days, which means heavy expenses. Those who have enough money to splurge add some more pomp and show to the basic ceremonies. Until recently, parents used to bear all the expenses of their children's weddings. Some time ago, men started the trend of taking on the expenses for their weddings themselves. Now women are also opting to defray the expenses incurred for their own wedding. They are either saving up for it, using their investments or taking wedding loans. Parents will still have to spend if their daughter is not working. But in the case of working women, it's the bride who is spending. I had a roommate in Mumbai who took a bank loan to fund her wedding. She said she did not want to burden her mother, who was a widow, with the expenses. This is a good trend. But if your parents are keen to share a part of the expenses, or want to spend on the whole wedding, let them. If you want, you can buy them something later, to make them comfortable in their old age. But do not make them feel bad by turning down their offer if they really insist. They may have saved for it and dreamed of it all though their lives. Let them realize their dreams.

- You may have planned and saved money for your marriage, but if your parents insist that they should spend, let them. It has do with emotions, you see.

If you are planning to bear the expense of your wedding yourself, you must have made concrete plans quite a few years before, and you must have started planning your finances from the day you started working. That sounds good. But I would still advise that you keep the expenses low. It hardly matters if you are getting married on an expensive chartered aircraft, or in the beautifully decorated ballroom of a hotel, or even in your own house if it's big enough. This is possible in small towns where houses are spacious, and usually not feasible in metropolitan cities where homes are small, cramped matchboxes. Do not plan a needless show of ostentation just because you want to impress people. Your goal should be to have a good celebration, where all the basic requirements are taken care of and the venue looks attractive. Work out the details of the event in such a way that it does not hurt your pocket. If you have to take a loan, let it be an amount which will not disturb your budget when you start repaying it. I will say again that you do not have to show off. Your aim is to have a decent wedding ceremony, which will not be not a burden on your bank balance.

- If you are spending on your wedding, make sure the expenses do not stretch beyond your means. It can be a low-key affair as long as it is presentable and makes people comfortable.

GIFTS

Too much serious stuff! Let's talk about gifts now. Well, yes, it's a wonderful feeling to get presents. But for a change, you may want to do something different about wedding gifts, like directing them to charity. Request your guests to give you cheques which are in the name of a particular orphanage or old-age home, or any other NGO. Though this is not a new idea, it has not caught on in India yet. So it remains reasonably new. You can try it out, and maybe you can make it go viral.

Anyway, if you decide to accept presents at your wedding, do make it a point to keep a record of who gave you what. This information should be strictly between you, your husband, his parents, and your parents. Do not discuss it with anyone else, because it may embarrass some relatives and friends. In case you are taking the charity route, you must hand over the envelopes to the institutions or organizations concerned without opening them and making a note of who donated how much. That would not be a very decent thing to do.

THE NUPTIAL SENSIBILITY THEORY—AND SOME THINGS TO REMEMBER

Marriage is a very important aspect of a woman's life. It's the start of a brand-new life for a woman, as she usually starts living with a new family and must strike up new relationships. You, while preparing for your wedding, should look at it with a sense of absolute responsibility. Don't just get married because the world tells you to. Apply and involve your mind and self in it. Be sensitive and handle the whole affair sensibly. By doing this, you will not just be making sure you are making the right decision for yourself, you will also be contributing towards saving many a female life, which is lost even before it begins. Slowly, people will stop looking at a girl as a financial burden and start seeing her as a self-dependent human being. For parents who cannot roll out millions for their children's weddings, the marriage of a girl will not mean inevitable social disgrace any more.

- You, as a bride, must say no to dowry. And insist on it. Also, make sure that your prospective in-laws and husband share your opinion.
- If you are working and intend to fund your wedding yourself, make sure you have made concrete plans. It must not disturb your financial stability.
- If your parents are eager to spend on your marriage, let them pitch in financially. If you stop them, you may be hurting their sentiments.
- Your prospective groom should not be earning less

than you. 'Less' means 40-50 per cent less than your salary.
- If you have a competitive streak, a husband earning more than you will be ruinous for your marriage. Marry someone earning less than you, someone less ambitious than you are, someone who has no problems with a wife who is more successful than him professionally. He will be able to admire you for your professional achievements with ease.
- Let the gifts from wedding guests go to charity.
- If you prefer to accept presents, keep the details of the gifts given strictly between yourself, your husband, your parents and your husband's parents.

5

The Wife

Some time ago, there was an advertisement on television where a man, talking about some family expense, says, 'That's managed by my finance minister.' He is referring to his wife. I have heard a lot of people, even finance experts, say, that women have proved the best financial planners. Look at the way our mothers and grandmothers, who were mostly housewives, managed their finances. I agree. The husbands handed over some part of their salaries, or sometimes the full amount, to their respective wives, and left it to them to manage all the domestic expenses. When the husband passed away, the wife gave in to fate and lived an austere life. This is what society expected from a widow. If she had children, she became financially dependent on them. This is just how things were.

Then, things changed. Women stepped out of their houses, professionals and housewives alike. They were out, either working, shopping, partying or travelling. They looked smarter. They talked smarter. But unfortunately, they had only stepped out of their houses, not their shells. Others, who broke their shells, went overboard. Yet another lot chose to live in their mothers' and grandmothers' era.

But it is high time wives got it right. Here are some real-life anecdotes followed by a talisman for wives to get their financial attitude right.

SHE WANTS TO KNOW, HE WON'T TELL

It was at one of our money psychology training sessions at a corporate house, that a woman voiced her concern about her husband and father-in-law not explaining anything about investments to her. One day when she was alone at home, she received a letter about a mutual fund statement. She tried reading it through, but was unable to decode some terms. When her husband and father-in-law returned in the evening and were discussing the stock markets after dinner, she asked them to decipher the terms mentioned in the statement and also explain all about mutual funds to her. Before she could even blink, she was told that it was not her cup of tea, and that she should go and make some coffee for the family. This incident obviously disappointed her.

The story left me startled for a while. It was difficult to come to terms with the fact that even a woman who would otherwise be considered 'independent' in every aspect could be told such a thing. However, she continued, she had come to our session to find out how to inform herself about personal finance. But, at the same time, she said that she was concerned that educating herself without the knowledge and approval of her male relatives could be seen as overstepping her boundaries.

- If your husband is reluctant to tutor you on the technical aspects of finance, help yourself. Find and read relevant literature. Watch relevant programmes on TV. Browse the internet.

I told the woman that she was not overstepping any limits. Educating oneself is always a positive development.

A woman I met at a financial planning conference some time ago did exactly that with her husband. Though she told me she was a housewife, she seemed quite well-up on financial matters. It's nice to see change happening, I thought to myself. But I realized a little later that the change was happening the wrong way. She told me, 'I fought with my husband every day for over a month till he handed over the login details of the demat account and our other investment accounts to me. I wouldn't give him any peace till I had all the details. I read everywhere that a housewife manages domestic budgets, and working wives manage both professional and domestic responsibilities. They should not be excluded from discussions about investments in their own home.'

If your male relatives are reluctant to explain finances to you, take a deep breath in, and a deep breath out. When you feel you have enough oxygen in your head...er, heart, start tutoring yourself in finance, without interrupting the household's peace and without hurting your male relatives' self-esteem. These days there is no dearth of easily accessible sources of information: the internet, newspapers, TV, magazines and books.

- If your male relatives are not willing to talk to you about finance, don't get aggressive about claiming your right to knowledge.

If you do not know how to operate the computer or go online, you probably have friends who can help you out. If you can access the internet, you will not need anything else. But if you are not comfortable with the computer, read relevant newspapers and magazines. If the men in your family are so actively involved in investments, they must subscribe to business and finance newspapers and magazines. Read them when you are free. Find out about relevant books and read them as well.

Now that you have an understanding of financial products and how they work, keep your knowledge to yourself unless there is a need to use it. Do not brag unnecessarily about your newfound know-how. It may hurt your male relatives' sentiments and cause unpleasantness within your family.

- When you are sufficiently educated, don't boast about your newly-acquired knowledge. You will hurt your man's self-esteem for no reason.

HE WANTS TO TELL, SHE WON'T LISTEN

There are stories galore about unwilling husbands and disgruntled wives when it comes to financial decision-making. But I have come across the opposite situation as well, where the husband wants his wife to learn about finance and budgeting, but the wife is reluctant as she finds it boring and unnecessary. A couple of years ago, I was on my way back to Mumbai after a small vacation in Jabalpur, my home town, and I had to catch a connecting flight in Delhi. When I got off the Jabalpur-Delhi flight, I found that the Delhi-Mumbai flight was delayed by a couple of hours due to bad weather in Mumbai. So, I decided to drop in to my cousin's home in Delhi.

At that time, I had just floated my company, and all family discussions were invariably centred on my start-up. That afternoon, as we spoke about *MoneyQuin*, my company's flagship brand, which is a money magazine for women, my cousin told me that her husband was always keen to explain financial matters to her. But she had always avoided the topic, thinking it would be boring.

Her husband then added that it had now become routine for him to suggest it every weekend, and for his wife to turn down the offer. Just for your information, my cousin is a well-placed professional with a BPO. I'm adding this to drive home the point that women who handle serious responsibilities at work, often involving big numbers and big money, can be averse to doing numbers on the personal front. My cousin said, 'I have left it to him,' in a tone that implied that she was giving her husband due importance.

Well, would it reduce your husband's 'importance' if you enhance your knowledge? I don't think so. In fact, ideally, he would be proud of you. Moreover, in my cousin's case, he was asking her to do so. If women in such positive environments don't make the effort, it is because of their laziness and regressive attitude, rather than their husband's ego. Pull up your socks. It's time.

- If your husband wants you to learn about finance, don't refuse. It's in your own best interest.

SHE DOESN'T CARE, HE CARES LESS

I have come across many couples where neither of the spouses is bothered whether or not the wife knows about 'official' financial planning, as against domestic financial management, where she is the boss. Life goes on without any worries, that is, until problems surface. Beware! Also, in many cases, both the husband and the wife are extremely careless about their finances. Neither knows what happens to their salaries during the month.

If you have married very early, perhaps in your mid-twenties, you can afford to be careless for the first couple of years. But if you are in your late twenties or in your thirties, you have to be judicious if you don't want to be taken unawares by rude shocks in the future. If your husband decides to set your finances in order, help him with the task. If you are the one who introduces method to the madness, make sure you talk your man into it.

- As a married couple, you can't afford to be careless in handling your money. Responsibilities can bog you down if your finances are not in place.

HER MONEY, POCKET MONEY

I was juggling all these thoughts while preparing for a training session at a reputed corporate house in Gurgaon. I happened to meet a marriage counsellor in the course of my preparations. While we talked, he mentioned one of his female clients who wanted a divorce because her husband wanted her to contribute a part of her salary towards family expenses. She strongly believed that her income was for her own expenses, while the family was to be taken care of by her husband's salary. When her husband objected to this, she responded that in India, we have a culture of housewives, where the household runs solely on the husband's salary, so why shouldn't theirs?

Fine, stick to that culture, quit your job and sit at home doing the sweeping, swabbing, and utensils. Will you? No? Then move with the revolution that you so fought hard to bring about. They call it women's liberation. I know you were one of the diehard rebels. So what's the problem now? You are earning too, and just like men, you also run the house. Go ahead. Make your contribution. Don't mistake 'women's liberation' for the freedom to detach from family life; Some women think that even if they live in a family, they have no role to play in it. A professor in Delhi, who was married to a man who works with a reputed pharmaceuticals company, walked out of the marriage when her mother-in-law asked her when they were planning to have children. The professor's argument was that she was independent and could not be questioned about her future plans!

- Your salary is not pocket money. Don't even imagine it that way.

YOURS, MINE, OURS

With another couple that I know, it was a different story. Both the wife and the husband were big spenders, and so, common household expenses like the electricity bill and the phone bill suffered. While they were enjoying their lives, the service provider decided to disconnect their telephone connection. Thus began the fight. They fought over financial responsibilities, as neither of them was ready to take on the 'burden'. They wanted to be independent. But what is this independence fraught with fights? Your goal should be to make life peaceful. Even if you want your independence, work it out in such a way that it does not upset your family budget and, more importantly, your relationship.

Just before you get married or as soon as you are married, your husband and you should open a joint account in a bank. Even while you do this, keep your individual accounts open. The next step is for the two of you to sit down together and plan how you will utilize your salaries. Your respective salaries need to each be divided into two parts—each month, one part will go to the joint account every month, and the other part will go to your individual accounts. You will have to divide your incomes between family and individual expenses, after estimating the expenses in each case. You will also need to prepare separate budgets for yourself and your family. Do this and see how smooth life becomes.

- A husband and wife should maintain three bank accounts—one individual account each, and one joint account for family expenses.

DO IT LIKE THIS

Our neighbours in Jabalpur own a flat in Chandigarh, which they have rented out to a family. This family of four—husband, wife and two children—has been living there for three years now. The wife is a lawyer, and works in the legal cell of a multinational company. She is extremely disciplined when it comes to managing finances. If the company allocates Rs 20,000 as house rent allowance, she will rent a house for Rs 18,000 per month, and use the rest of the money for water, electricity and other expenses.

She is so organized that our neighbours do not bother to run checks about the status of their flat. Their neighbours in Chandigarh tell them that the flat has the best interiors and exteriors in the whole lane, and it's the cleanest and best-kept house around.

Last year, while on their way to Mussoorie, they stopped at Chandigarh for a few hours to visit their flat. When they returned, they told us that the reports were right. The way a person manages money, can reveal a lot about her overall personality. It can also affect a family's lifestyle and the children's characters and their personalities. A man cannot run a family without a woman's support. So, if a woman fails to manage the budget of the family, the whole family will suffer. As wives, women must have their heads firmly placed on their shoulders, and think logically when it comes to money matters.

- As a wife, you can make or mar a family by the way you handle the finances.

DON'T BE A JERK

Here's another instance where the wife behaved stupidly, and the marriage went bust. A colleague of my brother went through a messy divorce a few years ago. He married a woman who he had known for three years beforehand; after they got married, she left her job. She was never very ambitious, and she always had plans to be a housewife. The problem began about a year after the wedding, when she started to demand things that were either unnecessary or that her husband could not afford. Case in point: for Diwali one year she wanted to buy twelve dresses and as many pairs of shoes. Her husband asked her, 'Doesn't it seem a bit too much? Let's buy two or three pairs right now, and then we can buy some more things later.'

She agreed, and they went out shopping. But as soon as they returned, she and called the police and registered a complaint that her husband was beating her. This happened every time her husband failed to fulfil her demands. Every second day he was taken away by the police and had to spend a night in the lock-up. This continued for a couple of months. He tried very hard to settle things. But nothing worked. So he applied for a divorce, which he was able to get three later. His wife refused to sign the papers all this while!

- If you are a compulsive spender, you will have to check this disorder after marriage. If your husband is a compulsive spender, he should check it too. If he does not, then you will have to leave him alone to his fate.
- If you are so obsessed with material possessions, don't leave your job. And try to work towards making a family, rather than ruining it. You have the skill and the power to do it. Use it. It's you who runs the world. It's a farce that it's a man's world. This false belief exists because of socio-political reasons. Wield your power. Put your head to work towards a progressive future, not a regressive and destructive one. It's all up to you—you and the money. The world will follow.
- As a wife, you are the one who calls the shots. Apply your intelligence positively, not destructively.

UNEMPLOYED HUSBANDS

The daughter of some family friends of ours married a man who came from a family that ran their own business. It was an arranged marriage. The bridegroom was also involved in the family business, or at least this was what the bride's family was made to believe. About six months after the wedding, we started hearing stories about how the husband refused to go to work, and insisted on staying at home instead. His excuse was that he was not enjoying work. At the same time, he never made any effort to find out what, if anything, he might enjoy doing. Basically, he gave up on life. The wife was a housewife until then; she had a postgraduate degree, but she didn't have any work experience.

A few months later, we heard she was expecting a child. Once the child was born, she started looking for a job, and ended up as an agent for a life insurance company. Three years later, they had another child. The husband was still home-bound. In fact, he never went back to work, and what's more, he never left his bed till he died. And I must not forget to tell you that he was an alcoholic. During the last few years before his death, he refused to leave his bed even to go the toilet. His wife nursed him through his self-imposed 'illness', raised their children, did the household chores, and went out selling insurance policies. I appreciate her for her dedication. But I have never felt like feeling sorry for her.

That's because I hold her completely responsible for everything she had to go through. When six months after her marriage, she found out the truth about her husband's professional status, she was advised by some of her friends and family to end the marriage. But she chose to agree with the handful of 'well-wishers', including her mother, that her husband was her life now. People, please, give me a break! If she had called off the marriage at that time, she could have had a better life by herself, or she could have found a better life partner.

- Moral of the story: avoid unemployed 'husband candidates'.

THE ALCOHOL CONNECTION

If you find a man who cannot live without drinking heavily for too long (even a week), who is not keen to work, reject him or give him six months to change. If he shows no commitment towards changing his ways, leave him. Do not think about the world.

Alcoholism will erode your family's finances to the point of no recovery. Besides, it aggravates frustration, turning it into anger which leads to violence in the family.

Drink is an expensive habit to cultivate. I know a very well-educated young man who used to lie to his mother and sister, and stay out at night on weekends, sometimes even on weekdays. One day he had plans with friends, but his sister had taken his car. She was a little late in returning and just as she returned, the car broke down out right outside the building gates. She told him, at which point he came rushing downstairs, banged into the car, and right in front of the security guards, rudely asked his elder sister to buzz off. After about half an hour he went back to the flat and took his frustration out on his mother. Didn't she know he was late for 'a group study meeting'? They had been getting together to 'study' for an exam for the past three years.

This young man was out of a job at the time. He had lost two consecutive jobs because of flaws in his character that he refused to work on. He was short of money, and his friends had stopped lending him money. He drank at his friends' expense. And anybody who told him that he should not be drinking so frequently, was his worst enemy, and he would even hit them on occasion. His two main 'enemies' at that time—his mother and his sister—were bearing all his expenses at the time. Rather than looking for a job and trying to improve his financial standards, he drank, shouted at, and beat up the women in the house.

After a year, his sister and mother were able to bring him back on the right track. Several people told his mother that all boys are like that. The only way to bring them back on track is to marry them off. So now they would present him as a 'sophisticated, organized, hard-working and eminently suitable boy' in front of the prospective bride and her family, and let his wife suffer later. Well, nobody can guarantee a person's chances of changing.

However, some people do change. They adapt to their surroundings, and if virtues are imposed on them, they accept them. So if you have been married to a man who has certain weaknesses which can ruin your family's budget and hence its future, give your man some time to improve. I have said elsewhere in this book as well, that women have a very strong sixth sense with which to judge people. Use it. Give him time. Then decide whether you want to stay or move on.

- Your husband's addiction to any sort of intoxicant can upset your family budget beyond repair. Leave him if he refuses to renounce his addiction.

ADDICTED WOMEN

It's not just about men and alcohol. We live in an era where women have equal access and equal inclination for alcohol, and even narcotics. One of my roommates' friends took to alcohol and weed in college. When she started working, she found this an easy escape from professional and personal stress. She had a boyfriend who did not know about this habit of hers. After a year of dating, they got married. Her husband's job required him to travel extensively and frequently, so she had many opportunities to indulge her stress-busting habit. But secrets have a short life, especially between married couples.

One time, her husband came back after a business trip to find that the IPTV (WiFi, telephone and television connection) bill of Rs 5,000 was not paid. Naturally, coming back to a silent television and phone, and a dysfunctional WiFi, he wanted to know what led to this. His wife told him she had no money! He was surprised that with her six-figure salary, she was unable to pay a piddling amount of Rs 5,000. A little investigation of what had happened to all her money, revealed the true story. He could not believe it. On emotional and moral grounds, he helped her start her rehabilitation. But two years later, she showed no signs of improvement. She had even escaped the rehab centre thrice. Some time later, they were divorced.

The husband was wise to have ended the marriage and left his wife to her fate. If he were to continue with the marriage, he would have ruined his own life.

Though I approve of the husband's decision in the above instance, I have observed that a wife who has an alcoholic or addicted husband would not leave him so easily. It is extremely unlikely that a housewife would have ended the marriage; and the chances of a working wife doing so are also low. Most wives would run the house single-handedly and try their very best to free their husbands of addiction.

- If you are an alcoholic or hooked to any other intoxicant, avoid getting married. Change your ways first, and then maybe you can make for a good wife.
- If you are addicted to intoxicants and have got married, talk about it with your husband and cooperate with your family when they try to help you out of the mess.

WOMEN WON'T LEAVE

Most housewives will even take up a job when a situation such as this arises. This is basically because of social pressure and the fear of losing a means of support, however illusionary it might be. According to our current social mentality, as long as a woman is living with her husband, she is safe and protected and is worthy of respect. The moment she steps out of the home for good, she loses all respect.

I would advise women to forget about all society's ossified beliefs when they are deciding about their future in difficult situations like the one above. Even if some people lose the respect they have for you when you leave an alcoholic husband, it will be won back in no time. People may go with the herd at the beginning, but once you have taken your bold decision, the world will eventually accept you.

- Women have more willpower than men. Rather than using your willpower to endure a life with an addicted, stubborn husband, move out and use it to build a better life for yourself and for your children.

WOMEN TAKE TO LAW…THE WRONG WAY

I once came across a case where someone's estranged wife had sent him a legal notice to pay for their eleven-year-old child's upbringing. This man had earlier offered to take care of all the child's expenses, and the mother had refused. Now she had come back through the legal route, which compelled the father to give fifty per cent of his salary to his wife for child maintenance. But this is very hard upon the man. If he gives half of his salary to his ex-wife, he will never be able to start a family again, or provide for his new family. The problem is that our laws are such that women get their way even if they are wrong.

I agree that these laws were put in place to help check atrocities against women. But sadly, they can be misused. Consider this. A distant relative's sister hated her mother-in-law because she was overly inquisitive. The mother-in-law liked giving advice even where it was not sought. The husband tried but failed to make his wife more tolerant, but she demanded that they shift to a separate house. After about a year of being married, she could not stand her mother-in-law any more and became so angry that she filed a dowry harassment complaint against her husband and mother-in-law.

I'll say it again. Please live with dignity and use your strong will in a positive way. Don't fight for power. You have to work towards living with your husband, rather than ruling over him. You have to build a family even as you guard your financial independence through proper understanding and knowledge.

STAND BY YOUR HUSBAND

Now I must tell you about another wife I grew up watching—my mother. My father did the budgeting every month, but he made sure that my mother was around when he was doing so. After him, my mother has continued the tradition. The pension that she gets is divided by and large on the same lines as my father would have, although some areas of expenditure have changed or are redundant.

My father's salary was divided under various heads like charity, children's school fees and stationary expenses, petrol, and household expenses which included our government-allotted ration, clothes, and groceries. My father was a government servant, so some expenses were already taken care of, for instance, that on the salary of domestic help. There was also an official car, but since my father was very strict about not using it for personal use, petrol expenses were included in the monthly budget. Financial investments didn't feature either, as during those times, lump sum investments in debt instruments were in vogue among the salaried middle class. My parents also always put away some money under the head of 'emergency'. Once the budget was drawn up, it was my mother who managed it. My father did not interfere thereafter.

When I grew up, one thing that I questioned was why my mother had never showed any interest in understanding financial investments. Although she knew where my father had invested and how much, she was never keen to understand the products. But that was how it was back in the 1980s. In fact now I think that my mother was quite ahead of her time. When my father passed away, and the details of the investment papers had to be changed, she was not completely at sea. She had at the ready all the documents and information required.

She kept a record of when and how much interest was earned on each investment, and when the premium stopped on their life insurance policies, even though she did not know how it all worked. Still, for her time, that was a lot. I come across a lot of women of my mother's generation who do not know even this much. They say, 'We already do so much work at home and office (if they are working housewives). Let the men do something too.' And everyone around laughs. But I fail to understand the joke.

Yes, life goes on. Even if you do nothing to change the status quo, time will go by. But you have a choice. You can choose to go where life takes you or conversely, you can learn some tricks and make your life turn onto your chosen route.

- Support your husband in financial management even if you are not very well-versed in the subject.

THE CRIB

While I am talking about you, 'the wife', let me not forget to tell you about the nag, who makes her husband feel bad by telling him that the work he does is beneath his dignity, and that the money he earns puts her in an embarrassing situation. I have a distant relative who owned an auto mechanic's shop in Delhi. His siblings were all better-off than him, in positions that were financially sounder than his. But I had never heard him complain about the work he did, even as he slogged it out from early morning to late at night, without making much money.

However, his wife complained constantly. As a child, I didn't know that society could be divided on the basis of money. It dawned on me as a teenager when I heard my aunt say about her husband, 'Everybody thinks we are no good just because we don't have enough money. I hate the work my husband does!' She wanted to wear expensive saris like her relatives. She hated travelling by public transport, and she wanted a car. But she knew they did not have the money for all these luxuries, and, frustrated, she blamed her husband.

I heard her say this quite a few times. Each time, I could see the helplessness on my uncle's face. I did not think that he deserved all this. Whenever he had the money, he did buy quality products for his family. But my aunt wanted to live in absolute luxury.

As their children grew up, it was not only the wife who was embarrassed about her husband's profession. Once, I heard their son telling his friend, 'My father is an engineer!' Well!

It was then that I started looking at my relatives in terms of social strata. Initially, I thought my uncle was a failure, a lazy man who did not want to progress in life. Later, I tried understanding what leads people to stay in situations like my uncle's. I realized that it had a lot to do with the environment my uncle had grown up in.

I strongly believe that if a person cannot grow or succeed to a reasonable level, it is because of lack of effort and will. But I also believe that a strong will and being able to make the effort to achieve your goals are a function of your environment and its effect on your psyche. People in bad environments have to make more effort to develop a strong will, so as to help them succeed in life.

Mothers may be controlling or nagging by nature, or as a result of circumstances. Sometimes the mother is not treated well by her in-laws, and since she cannot speak up in front of them, she takes her frustration out on her children by frequently beating them or scolding them for no reason. These children, owing to the constant and unhealthy emotional trauma, frequently grow up to be non-achievers.

My aunt should have tried to understand the reason behind her husband's sluggish growth. Besides, she, and many other women in such situations, should sit down and draft a budget for the family's income, rather than using their time and energy to make their husbands feel like losers. My aunt had never properly budgeted the small income that my uncle made from his business. On the contrary, she would often ignore the budgets he would draw up, saying, 'A budget for such a small income is a joke.' Had she made a budget and stuck to it rather than spending her time nagging, they would have been able to improve their financial position sooner or later.

- Respect whatever your husband earns. Don't crib about a small income. Manage it well.

THE RATIONAL AGGRESSION THEORY—AND SOME THINGS TO REMEMBER

As a wife, be aggressive but let there be some rationale to it. Be mad, but apply method to it. Show your aggression in your desire to learn and know. But don't go crazy if your desire is not fulfilled in the way you want. If things are not going as they should be, you cannot pick up a sword and go around chopping random off people's heads. If your money is not being handled right by your husband, or if you are stranded at the end of a tragic play, it's your fault. Mend your ways, aggressively yet rationally. I stress the word rational because you must do all this without hurting your man's ego. You are not doing all this to destroy your marriage, but to better it. So, let's see what this theory expects you to do.

- Keep yourself updated about financial matters even if your male relative continues to do the fieldwork for investments and financial planning.

- If your male relatives ignore your numerous requests to explain investments to you, no need to get violent. Tutor yourself.
- Make a budget for your family.
- Think and act logically. Do not go back to your ex-husband demanding money for yourself or for your child's upkeep, with the intention of sabotaging his future. Nothing is more disgraceful than being a sadist.
- Refrain from revealing all your financial information to your husband and your in-laws until you know them very well, and until you know that they will treat your money as their own, that they will not use it carelessly.
- If your husband is over-spending on alcohol or drugs even as the household expenses suffer, talk to him and give him six months to cut down on or give up these habits. If he refuses, time to pack up your bags and walk out. Do not forget to take your children along. They have no future with an alcoholic.
- If you are constantly reminding your husband about his weak financial status, remember that you will come off as a nag and it will do nothing to improve the situation. It will only lead to more unpleasant moments in your family. Rather, take charge and figure out ways to improve your family's financial status along with your husband.
- If you have previously been on good terms with your in-laws, aside from the routine hiccups in every family,

then you must continue your material interactions like giving gifts etc after your husband's demise. Do not go by what other people and your children have to say.

Remember, your goal is to keep the game going. There are no winners and losers in this game of roulette. So, just play it!

6

The Mother

I could write reams on this subject—a mother's role in shaping a person's money quotient. I have observed that however far we may have come, when it comes to rearing children it's still the mother who takes centre stage.

One of my brother's neighbours in Delhi is the mother of a six-year-old girl. When I visited Delhi, I became good friends with her. She is almost a single mother. Her husband worked in Bangalore for three years before moving to Mauritius in 2011. Whenever he is in Delhi, which is for a week at a time, his time is taken up by his friends. I have seen them hanging out in the neighbourhood, smoking and chatting over drinks. Every year he takes a bike trip to Leh, Ladakh and Mussoorie, with his friends. His wife never goes along, because she cannot leave the child behind. Although her in-laws live in the block next to ours, she finds it awkward to leave her child with them for a fortnight. She says, 'It would be very mean to leave the child with them and go out to have fun.' Right. Now imagine a husband babysitting while the mother goes on holiday with her gang of friends! I have never yet come across such a family.

Money being an important aspect of a child's overall growth, mothers have to know their tricks well. In addition, it is becoming difficult to manage children's financial needs in our new culture where we are all trying to walk the fine line between not curbing our children's desires and not giving them too much freedom too early. This chapter is a guide for mothers who want to know where to draw the line.

A neighbour dropped by one evening to spend some time with my mother in Jabalpur. I could hear them from the living room where I sat working, which is not very far from the lawn where my mother and her pal were enjoying the spring evening. Just then I heard the neighbour's eight-year-old son shouting, 'Mom, give me money. I want to buy chocolate. Give me twenty rupees.' His mother refused, saying she had given him twenty rupees in the morning. The son said he had spent that on candy. She refused to give him any more money, and the boy started to create a fuss, yelling and pretending to cry. His mother got up and slapped him. My mother tried to stop this circus happening in our lawn, but she was not able to.

The mother explained that she had to do this more and more often, because her son had been demanding money more frequently. She went on, 'His father does not care. He comes home at night and gives him fifty rupees if he asks for twenty. His grandmother also feels happy when he asks her for money; she tries to show her love for him by giving him money, and in the course of all this, he is getting spoilt.' Well, she was right. Grandmothers and fathers have a particular behaviour pattern which we call 'Perpetual Gratitude': they never say no when children ask them for money so that the children are always happy—and they are gratified by this.

My mother told the neighbour that she could buy him chocolate herself, if she does not want to give him any more cash. But she replied that it was difficult for her to fulfil all his demands, as they were not restricted to merely chocolate and candy. Today it was chocolate, tomorrow it would be a new toy. She also said that she was a little confused. She wanted to allow her son to be independent, but she could not figure out how loose she should leave the reins and when she should pull back.

Well, it's a good idea to make your children independent. But the execution will need some intelligence. Tell your husband or mother or mother in-law that their habit of handing out money to the child is harming her or him. But from my experience, it's unlikely that they will understand your point. So your job is to make sure that the money they give your child is utilized properly.

It's easy to teach the value of money to pre-teens because their minds are malleable, and they can be moulded in any direction. You will have to undo a lot of things along with doing a lot of new things. To begin with, avoid the cane or the slap. It creates unnecessary drama and unhappiness.

Also, physical punishment can make the child stubborn. So, even if you occasionally get annoyed, no physical violence please. It was not the cane that taught my brother and me the value of money, but the process of growing up watching our parents' smart money management.

- Avoid physical punishment and yelling, even if your child demands money all the time.

I must tell you about a trick my mother would play on us. When we asked her for pencils or any other stationery, she would ask us to kneel down in the prayer corner, fold our hands, shut our eyes and pray to God to give us what we needed. When we opened our eyes at our mother's signal, the pencils would be right in front of us. Sometimes, if we had been careless and lost our things at school, 'God' would not replace them, despite our prayers. The reason, our mother explained, was that 'God' gets annoyed with children who do not take care of their things and lose them.

You may feel that such tricks would not work in today's times. Yes, definitely you cannot trick children these days into believing that if they close their eyes and pray, God will drop by and give them a new notebook. But you can tell them to pray to get what they want, and later when they are asleep, slip it into their school bags or cupboards. Of course, you cannot get them anything that they 'pray' for. If a twelve-year-old boy prays for a motorbike, of course you shouldn't drive one home the next day. But just so that they do not lose faith in your little trick, tell them that God will give it to them when they grow up. Tell them, 'If he gives you everything now, you will have nothing to play with when you grow up.' You can even rope in your children's favourite cartoon characters or Santa Claus to help you out.

The idea is to make your children realize that money is not easy to acquire. It requires effort, and if they tend to lose their possessions or if they are careless about their money too often, God or their 'friend' gets upset.

- Children must realize that money is not easy to get. It requires effort.

My brother and I never got pocket money while we were growing up, although we were given some money when we went to school, and later, to college. This was always sufficient, since I do not recall any instance when the money was not enough for our expenses. In fact, we did not have very big expenses, and if we needed something extra, my parents would get it for us.

Sometimes we got pleasant surprises as well. Once, after watching the movie *Maine Pyar Kiya*, when we came out of the theatre, I told my family how good the songs had been. Then I turned to my father and said, 'Papa, let's get the (audio) cassette of these songs.' It seemed my parents also liked the songs, because I remember my father immediately smiled at my 'demand' and looking at my mother, said, 'See what she's saying.' My mother also smiled. The next day when I returned from school, I went into my room as usual. Suddenly I heard music. It was the title track of *Maine Pyar Kiya*! I ran out to the living room where the music system was. It was lunch time, and my father was home too. He had bought the cassette on his way back from office. Beautiful surprise!

These days, parents find it tough to tackle the topic of

pocket money. What we need here is smartness, especially on the part of the mother. Fathers, if they are earning well, do not mind giving their kids whatever they can pull out of their wallets.

However, if handled intelligently, pocket money is the best first step towards a youngster's money education. The first smart move is to give her or him the pocket money as a reward for something—for something he or she enjoys doing, or for something which he or she must learn as a part of growing up. It could be for helping in the kitchen, teaching their grandparents how to use the computer, teaching the maid's children, or even for getting good grades or some other achievement in school.

- Pocket money is the best way of teaching children the value of money.

I would like to put in a word of caution here. If you tell children that they will get pocket money only if they get good grades in class or win a competition, you are cultivating a winner-loser mentality in them. I am not in favour of this trend, which is quite prevalent in our schools. In this winner-loser arrangement, children become obsessed with beating others and making it to the top spot. It's the outcome that matters more to them, rather than the learning that goes into it.

To avoid this, you can conduct your own little casual tests at home to check their understanding of a subject. If they are not good in a particular subject, have them study and understand only as much as they need to pass their tests and exams. Imposing something on them which they do not like will do no good. You must have seen yourself that most of what you studied in school, and even in college, is of no use now. I agree that schools shape our personalities, but only when you stress on learning rather than the results.

So why make your children miserable by forcing them to do something they dislike, just because it gives you an opportunity to boast to your friends? If you find out that your child is doing well in certain subjects, let him or her devote more time to those particular subjects. For the rest of them, allow them to put in as much effort as they need to get through their examinations.

I really enjoyed my English class in school. I used to look forward to it every day. When I reached high school, it became even more interesting as I had one of the best English teachers I have ever known. Ms Jenny helped me realize that I was in love with the subject. I used to enjoy 'playing with words', and it gave me a high when I wrote something of my own. I read Shakespeare, Maugham, Wordsworth, Agatha Christie and Gerald Durrell with equal ease. But sadly, English was only a back-up subject. We had to have good grades in the sciences and the social sciences to get an impressive aggregate grade. So, I got a chance to spend some time with my favourite subject only during the holidays. The rest of the time, being a science student, I was crunching numbers or deciphering chemical reactions or devouring historical hierarchies.

During my final year of college, I started studying for the Civil Services exam. Although I never took the exam, the reading of various subjects like history, anthropology, science, English, and Hindi, that was part of preparing for these examinations, did a lot to widen my outlook. As time passed I developed a more evolved perspective and enriched my knowledge. Studying for those exams introduced me to new literature and writers that I would have never come across otherwise, new cultures, and an insight into my own culture, the world's history and evolution.

This is what education should actually be. It should be a process of learning rather than a means to make it to the winner's podium. It should encourage minds to explore. If you have ever read *My Family and Other Animals* by Gerald Durrell, you would know that he explored the flora and fauna around his place on the Greek island not because he was preparing to be an ace scientist but because he simply enjoyed it.

- Make learners out of your children rather than winners and losers.

All children are inquisitive. But as their minds get crowded with all the things offered by our education system and our society, they tend to lose this attribute.

I hope I have made clear the difference clear between learning for learning's sake, and learning for achievement's sake. Try to test whether your children know their subjects well and whether they are able to apply logic. If they can, even if they are unable to make it to the top positions at school, tell them they are good because they have learnt their subject well. So they get pocket money. The winner-loser mentality can be really harmful for your child's professional and personal growth later in life. They will grow up fighting for the top slot without valuing knowledge. They may even apply underhand means to get to the top, if winning is all that matters to them.

- Give your children pocket money if they have learnt their subjects well, and not only if they bring back good grades through rote learning.

This practice will help inculcate discipline and learning among your children. But just as you periodically get a bonus at work, let your children have a little bonus sometimes. They should not grow up thinking that everything sells and that they will get monetary gain from whatever they do. If they do, they will never believe that some things should be done for goodwill and charity.

- It's good to make your children 'earn' pocket money, but don't always give it to them in return for something. This will lead them to think that everything in the world is to be done for money.

Another step towards ensuring smart pocket money management is to spend quality time with your children. A seven-year-old girl living in my friend's building in Delhi goes around ringing the doorbells of houses of people who are friendly with her. She makes these flying visits to ask for toys. Once when I was visiting my friend, this girl met me and struck up a conversation. We chatted a couple of times. I liked her for her chirpiness. I had a toy camera with me, which I presented to her. The next day the doorbell rang again. It was the same little girl. As soon as I opened the door, she said, 'You said you will give me a Barbie doll. I have come to take it.' Since it was the first time, I thought she may just not know how to start a conversation, so I let her in and offered her a cold drink. She drank it, and then left. As she was leaving, she told me, 'You get the Barbie. I will come tomorrow.' And she did come back. Her best friend in the building has a room full of Barbie dolls, so she wanted some too.

A week later, she came again asking for some other toy. This time, I gave her a chocolate and let her go. Both her parents were working and her nanny was quite lax and inattentive to her. Although this girl's grandparents lived nearby, she didn't visit them very often, as her mother was not on very good terms with them. When at home, the parents spent their time fighting over who should look after the child, and eventually and obviously, it was always concluded that it was the mother's responsibility. But neither knew how to do it along with the requirements of their job.

- Pocket money makes for a good learning tool for children only when you spend quality time with your children, and tell them how it should be used.
- Working mothers have to consider it a part of their routine to be with their children after work. (The same goes for working fathers too, of course.)

Some time ago, I met the six-year-old niece of a friend of mine in Delhi. This little girl was in the habit of lifting things from peoples' houses. Her mother is a major in the army, and they live in Siliguri. They were in Delhi on vacation. One day when I was visiting my friend, the girl's mother had left her there and had gone out shopping. My friend told me that when the little girl would leave in the evening, she would invariably take some of her cosmetics or her daughter's toys along with her. She had to hide her daughter's toys because if her niece takes them, her daughter cries foul, and the girls end up fighting.

In such cases, where the mother cannot leave her job, she should make it a point to spend quality time with her children when she gets home from work. You can easily relax for an hour or finish the household work in an hour, and then no matter how tired you are, you must spend time with their children.

If parents, especially mothers, spend more time with their children, the children will be less attracted to material things. You will see an automatic decline in their demand for toys and treats. Talk to them about their day at school and after school, about friends and studies. Children seek company. If they do not get it from their parents, they look for it in toys or the TV. When they are bored of those, they go wandering about to neighbours' or relatives' houses. Consider it a part of your job to spend time with your child.

- When parents spend more time with their children, they are less attracted to money and material things.

Now, let's move a step further. Everything that we discussed above will work very well for your pre-teen children. But you will have to rework your strategies as your children become teenagers. The teenage years are a very crucial patch in the lives of children and their parents. Teenagers go through major emotional imbalances, and parents have to be extra-careful while dealing with them. One very common problem seen among teenagers is credit abuse. They borrow frequently without thinking about repaying, mostly from friends and outsiders. They feel awkward about taking too much money from their parents, as they think that they are grown-up enough to not depend on their parents.

One weekend when my mother was visiting me in Mumbai, she hung up the phone after a long conversation with one of her friends. This woman told my mother that the parents of two of her son's friends had come calling that morning. They had said that her son had borrowed money from them and was being evasive about returning it. His father beat him up in front of the visitors.

The son said that he had borrowed money to buy a PlayStation. When he had asked his parents for the money they said they did not have so much money to spare for a game. He said he was disappointed because his friends said, 'Your father has built such a big house. He must have a lot of money. If he does not give you any, that means he doesn't love you.'

The reality was that his father was a salaried employee. To buy this piece of property, he had saved up all his life and taken a small loan to meet the expenses incurred on first buying the plot of land and then constructing a house on it. The parents refused to give him money for a PlayStation because they could not afford it. But the teenager would not understand this. He argued with them often, and these arguments culminated in loud fights. My mother's friend was also worried about her twelve-year-old daughter who was witness to all this domestic chaos.

The sad part is that even if they are taught the right money lessons as children, most teenagers tend to forget these lessons as soon as they hit their teens. Early adolescents can still be moulded the way you want, but teenagers will resent you if they get a whiff of any effort to change their ways and thinking. They have to be handled subtly. Amazingly, fathers are usually tough with teenage sons, but they are friendly with their teenage daughters, while teenage sons open up easily to their mothers, and teenage daughters can easily hate their mothers for being overprotective. But at the end of the day, teenage daughters also find more comfort with their mothers. So it's the mother who plays the most pivotal role in moulding her teenage children and fathers must follow her lead.

- No matter how much you teach your children about money management, most tend to forget these lessons as soon as they hit the teenage years.

To begin with, talk to your teenage children often. Involve them in household conversations. They must know the family cash flow situation. No need to reveal your investments, insurance, and important budgets to them, of course, because they are still too young to understand their significance. It may look like a lot of surplus money to them, and they may fight with you to give it to them for fulfilling their needs. So tell them almost everything. They should know how a house is run, that there is no magic trick to get money, and the only way is sweat. They must know how their parents slog it out to earn money.

- Open up to your teenagers. They should know how a house is run and how money is earned.

Secondly, encourage them to find part-time jobs like giving tuitions, waiting at a coffee shop, or any other job that they would enjoy doing. When they start getting their own salary, teach them about budgeting. Make a simple table with four sections—Charity, Saving, Essentials and Fun. Their salaries must be divided under these four heads. They must learn the importance of giving (charity) and saving while they are still at an impressionable age. They must also know the significance of needs (essentials) and wants (fun) right now.

- Let your teenagers find vocational jobs. It will give them firsthand lessons in money management.

If you manage to bring your teen children so far, you will have crossed a big hurdle. They will never forget the lessons they learnt in their teens, and they will carry them forward to the next generation.

Yet another thing which you have to teach your children at this age is the ethics of borrowing. You must tell them about credit abuse. This is the age when children tend to borrow heavily even if they get enough money at home.

This is largely because they are acquiring habits like smoking and drinking, and they are being exposed to new expensive gadgets, motorbikes and cars, which some of their richer friends may already have. They need money very frequently to satisfy these wants. Since they think their parents have no idea about their new adventures, they refrain from asking them for money frequently. Hence the borrowing. Once they start earning their own money, they may stop borrowing if they are not too hooked to smoking, drinking, partying and splurging.

As a teenager's mother, you need to be very alert. Do not make it obvious that you are keeping an eye on them. Ask your children to invite their friends over more often. When the gang is there, be a part of it. Don't try to come across as too cool, which will only embarrass your teenage children. Act your age, but be friendly with your young guests. A mother's involvement in a calculated and positive way in their lives can keep teenagers away from addictions and from wasting money.

- Your teenager must know the adverse fallout of credit abuse. Talk to them about this.

A family I was very close to in Mumbai had sent their son to study advertising at a prestigious school in the US. They had spent a lot of money on his course and his living expenses abroad, but they got a shock when the school expelled him for objectionable behaviour, and sent the nineteen-year-old back home. The father was very angry, but the mother stopped him from expressing this to his son, fearing that the son might resort to doing something stupid and dangerous. So nobody said anything to him. The mother thought her son was adult enough to understand that what had happened was wrong, and that he would do the right thing from now on.

But what followed was an increasing demand for money. After three months, the nineteen-year-old declared that he was planning to start a business, for which he needed two lakh rupees. Although the father was not very keen on giving him this money, the mother agreed on the grounds that her son had had to face so many things at such a young age, and that he should not feel depressed any more. So the father gave in. Barely a month later, the update was that the son's 'business partner' had disappeared into thin air... along with the money. Well, the right thing to do at this point was to have a conversation. The couple tried, but it did not work.

- If you have a dropout teenager, no need to take pity on them. Send them out to struggle.
- Talk to them, and if talking does not help, ask for help from an outsider, as this may make more of an impression on your teenagers.

In such a situation, it is best to get outside intervention. I have seen that teenagers are more influenced by people they meet outside their families. They will be more ready to listen to a teacher they admire, rather than their own parents, even if they are trying to tell them the same thing. Get someone to counsel your kid. Let it be someone who your teenager child knows and admires. If you are able to bring your children on the right track while they are still teenagers, you will have saved yourself and your children of a lot of trouble later.

I lived in a studio apartment when I worked in Delhi a few years ago. The landlady, a sixty-something widow, lived with her thirty-something son on the floor below. I would occasionally hear the duo arguing, although I could never really make out what the argument was about. Sometimes there were heated quarrels. One morning, when I went to pay the rent, I was witness to one of these quarrels. The landlady asked me to sit down while she saw her son off.

She had asked her son to get some groceries. She had already taken out the money from her cupboard, and put it on the table, ready to give it to him. He came out of his room with a preoccupied look on his face, and, without acknowledging my presence, went straight to the table and counted the money. And whoa! I was startled! The son began yelling at his mother that she gave him only trifling sums of money. He said, 'You think I will spend your money on myself. Get this straight: I have very caring friends who are there to take care of my needs. I don't need your money.'

The mother replied that she had never thought any such thing, and that he could always ask for more money if he needed it; she had never refused. To this, he retorted that she didn't have to worry about him, and that she did not need to announce to outsiders that he was taking money from her. She could keep it all, he ended, and left the house in a huff.

Her son had finished a course in cinematography from

a prestigious institute in the US. It had been an expensive course and he had paid for it with an education loan. He aspired to be a fashion cinematographer. He had expected to get a break immediately, what with his 'wide network' of contacts in the field. But alas, the 'wide network' turned out to be a mirage, as it always does just when you are all set to fall back on it. Close friends and family suggested that he get another job as a stopgap arrangement. But he refused, on the grounds that he wanted to 'single-mindedly work towards achieving his goal'. If he started working elsewhere, it would divert him and he would not get the time to work towards his ambition. Fair enough! So people assumed that he was working towards achieving his goal. And this was how he was going about it. His days were spent sleeping and watching television, shouting at his mother or occasionally, chasing the 'influential people' who had promised to get him his dream job. His nights were spent drinking and smoking with friends who were also 'struggling' in some field or the other. Unable to fulfil his ambition and, at thirty, still struggling to figure out the right money attitude, he was mostly found squandering his time. His mother was a mute observer to all this. She did all the household chores as the luxury of a maid had to be discontinued, considering their dwindling funds. The son would not assist her in any household work as he 'did not do all this kind of work'. During lighter conversations, he would tell his mother that she didn't have to bother either. Eventually he would be rich and he would take good care of her. Well, the mother could only pray that this day came sooner rather than later.

In situations like these, it's best to ask someone outside the immediate family for help. Some close family friend or relative, whom you can trust to handle such situations with finesse, can be brought in. You should also be sure that your child relates to this person easily. In the case of daughters in similar situations, the mother herself can be a good counsellor. Daughters generally do not land in such situations as they pull up their socks much earlier, but if your daughter proves to be an exception, you can double up as a counsellor.

Communication is the best way to begin. Be her friend. Think like a teenager of today, but do not try to become one. Teenagers, and especially teenage daughters, hate to see their mothers trying to act too cool. They think their mothers are trying to attract attention, now that they are old and nobody looks at them any more. So try to understand the teenage psyche, think like them, and even mingle with them. But act your age. If you start doing what they are doing, then you will lose your authority. For instance, if your teenager daughter is smoking and you want her to stop, mingling with her gang and taking to smoking yourself will be counter-productive. Besides, she will not take you seriously about anything after that. Most daughters think emotionally, and even if they stray when they are younger, they get back on track as they grow up. And they are not averse to listening if you communicate with them.

- It's easier to connect with teenage daughters than teenage sons. Understanding teenage boys takes some effort. They are more volatile in their thoughts and behaviour compared to their female counterparts.

I must tell you about these three sisters I have known ever since they were teenagers. When they reached their teens, they instantly caught everybody's attention for two reasons. First, all three of them were stunningly beautiful, and second, they were always out and about. You would never find them at home. Although their parents were not very well-to-do, these girls always had money to splurge and were always very well-dressed. They would even drop in at their relatives' places and directly ask for money. While some relatives obliged a couple of times, some others simply turned them down.

The girls were in their teens, the most unstable patch in a human being's life. The eldest was eighteen years old, the middle sister was seventeen, and the youngest was fifteen years old. When the eldest daughter turned nineteen, their mother passed away. It was freedom for all now. A year later, when things started getting out of hand, their maternal grandmother pitched in, and married off the eldest daughter who was then twenty years old.

She married a man who ran a small shop in a fairly shabby area of Delhi. If she had been given proper guidance and had achieved something in her life, she would have been married to a man also doing something better in his life. However, after her marriage she got her act together under her grandmother's guidance. She found a job with a BPO two years after her marriage. Her husband still runs the shop, but it is now in a different, more advantageous location. Their standard of living has only become better over the years. It has been ten years since their marriage, and they have two sons.

The second sister is single and working as a team leader with a reputed multinational company. A few years ago, the youngest sister got married to a banker.

Women set their house in order sooner or later, even without guidance. This is because women are emotionally stronger than men, and they can weather the storm and bounce right back. But men, being emotionally weaker, need emotional support from women to keep them going. Men need women to complete them. Women can live very good and impressive lives as single mothers and single professionals, without any support from men. Well, yes, women who wish to be mothers do need men to fulfil their desire. But other than that, they can pull it all off pretty single-handedly.

Anyway, so if you are the mother of a teenage son or an older struggling son, you will need to put in more effort to keep him on track. You will need to think intelligently and use wise tactics. And, yes, if you thought I had shifted focus away from the subject of money, I have not. All the problems that you face as a mother are by and large related to money. You might say that your children getting involved in unsuitable love affairs has nothing to do with money. I say, ask yourself the reasons why you are calling the affair unsuitable. I can tell you the most common and probable reasons. You might reject your daughter's choice of spouse because the man is not well-established in his career, which is another way of saying that he does not earn enough money. You may also be unhappy with your son's choice because the girl may not belong to a rich family, or because she earns more than your son does. Isn't all this related to money?

So, as a mother, mould your children's money attitude properly, and the rest will follow. I leave you on a positive note, with a story about my own mother.

There was a time in my life when I was going through a financial crunch. My brother's birthday was round the corner, and I told my mother that I could not afford a decent gift for him this time, I just didn't have the money for it. She immediately said, 'Never say that you don't have money. Even if you are in the red, say you have enough.' Initially, I didn't understand the logic behind this. Nevertheless, I decided to try it and I felt it did have a strong psychological effect. I bought a nice but not very expensive gift for my brother that year, which he was really happy to receive. And I never really ran out of money after I adopted this attitude. I have also noticed that people who go around telling the world about their empty coffers don't leave a very good impression. At times, listeners even think that they are indirectly asking for money by whining about their financial status.

Somehow, my parents were always right about money matters. They taught me and my brother exactly the lessons that would help us make our lives financially better, and amazingly I realize that these lessons are valid for the next generation as well. There was one idiom my mother used to say quite often. This Punjabi idiom can be translated as 'Even the uneducated have money. It's your knowledge that matters, not money. So work hard and study.' It means that if you educate yourself, money will follow. People will hold you in higher regard if you are well-read and rich.

But she never really explained this proverb, so this is how I initially viewed it: 'So what if I do not have money? I will be rich with all the knowledge that I gain. People are respected for their knowledge, not their money.' But I was wrong. The result of this perception was that with my first couple of job offers, I did not negotiate for a better pay package than what was being offered to me. But later on, when I got to know my colleagues, I realized that negotiating one's salary is very much the norm.

- Tell your child that money is very important in life, but it must be earned by the right means.

And last but not least, as a mother, refrain from giving your married daughter too much advice too often. As far as possible, stay out of her life. I have noticed that wherever a mother is actively involved in her married daughter's household, there are problems. At times, too much interference by the mother in her daughter's married life leads to the splitting up of the daughter's joint family. This happens because you, as a mother, tend to see only your daughter's interests. Unwittingly, you tend to look at her in-laws as outsiders who are not being fair to your daughter. And you do this as an external individual who is not an active observer present on the spot. So, your perception is based more on imagination or hearsay than on reality. Assumptions are always dangerous.

Keep a safe distance from your married daughter's life. You should be confident that you have done your bit to prepare your daughter to take on life. Let her manage it on her own. Do not let her be dependent on you for every little thing. Let her give her mother-in-law that status in her life now. You will help bring her closer to her husband's family by keeping out of her daily life.

THE RELATIONAL TRANSDUCTION THEORY— AND SOME THINGS TO REMEMBER

All that we discussed above is part of the Relational Transduction Theory. In your capacity as a mother, a relationship which makes you the closest observer and mentor of your children, you transfer your positive energies and attitude to your children. This can apply to anything. But as we have seen, everything revolves around money. So, this theory is about transferring to your children your positive thoughts and energies related to money, in order to ensure a better future for them.

- Avoid physical punishment. Get angry if you really must. But avoid hitting your children; it may lead them to develop habits like stealing and borrowing in the long run.
- Spend quality time with your children. If they get enough of your time and attention, they will be less attracted to anything that money can buy.

- Give them pocket money as a reward for something well-learnt rather than well-done.
- Sometimes, give them pocket money as a little bonus. They must know that not everything is done for material gain.
- Teach them the value of money through simple tricks.
- Teach them budgeting.
- Make sure that the money they are getting is being utilized the right way.
- With your teenage daughter, have a heart-to-heart conversation. For your teenage son, you might need external help from a close relative, a teacher or a friend whom your son looks up to.
- For your adult struggling son again you will need someone to counsel him. It may be a family friend who is wise enough to tackle such men and situations. It may also be his girlfriend, if you think she is mature enough. But it must be someone whom your son is comfortable connecting with.
- Let your married daughter fight her own wars. Your pitching in as a warrior behind her will only spoil her relationships with her in-laws.

7

The Mother of a Special Needs Child

A mother's role is challenging and demanding in even the most ordinary circumstances. But being the mother of special children with limitations and below ordinary abilities comes with added challenges and responsibilities. Special children are often slow learners. And they are not treated well by other children, and even by adults, because they are different. Most often, prejudices set in, and these children are ostracized.

During my research while writing this book, I realized that in bringing up special children, male or female, the second most important step the parents take is to make them financially independent. One mother of a special child told me, 'Ever since my boy learnt how to count numbers and identify currency, I feel secure about him.'

Other children learn number crunching at school, and they do it faster. But with special children you need to be more thoughtful and involved. They do not grow up learning calculations and numbers like your other children. They perceive things on a different wavelength. And I address this chapter specifically to mothers of special children because, as I said in another chapter, mothers are closer to children, as compared to fathers.

- Mothers of special needs children face special challenges and responsibilities in bringing up their children.

I have known two special people well. One was my neighbour in Jabalpur and another was my own aunt, my father's youngest sister. Both were epileptic, affected with tonic-clonic seizures. My aunt passed away in 2010, while my neighbour passed away a year ago.

Even with her disorder, my aunt had the most disciplined routine among all her siblings. She got up at the same time every morning, had a bath, and combed her thick, black, waist-length hair into a tight plait. It was a big joint family which comprised the nuclear families of two of my father's brothers, my grandparents, my father's three unmarried sisters and one unmarried brother. My own small family lived separately in the office bungalow allotted to my father. We visited our extended family twice or thrice every week.

Sometimes while playing with my cousins I would misplace my things. Once, for instance, I left my new hair band in the barn, where we had been playing. By the time we left, I was too tired to realize that my hair was all over the place, and that the hair band was missing. My mother did not notice at first either, but when she did, she said that if my aunt saw it, it would not be lost. She said this whenever I forgot things there, and she was always right.

Yes, my aunt, despite her disorder, was very organized. She had one small iron trunk in which she kept all her belongings. All her clothes were always spick-and-span, and neatly folded in the trunk. She was offered a cupboard for her things many times, but there was something about the trunk which never let her give it away. If she happened to find anything that we had forgotten when we had visited, she would put it safely in her trunk, and hand it over to us when we visited the next time. And if she did not spot our things, they were lost forever. Nobody else was this careful and concerned in the whole family. She kept her little room and trunk very tidy. I must remark here that my grandmother had little to do with all this. My aunt managed it herself; in fact, she was tidier than my grandmother.

Later, when all my father's siblings were married, my grandmother and my uncle had the bright idea to have this aunt married off as well. My uncle thought that marrying her off would reduce some burden on him after his parents had passed away. My grandmother thought her daughter would get a better life, where she would not be dependent on her siblings. Everybody agreed, except my parents and my father's aunt, one of my grandmother's sisters, who was then the principal of a school in Jabalpur. My father's aunt proposed a very intelligent and feasible alternative. She suggested that my grandparents create a fixed deposit for their daughter, rather than marrying her off. The fixed deposit would make her financially independent and she would not be dependent on anyone after her parents were gone. My parents supported this idea, but the rest of the family ignored this advice, and went ahead with the marriage plans anyway.

One of my grandparents' neighbours had a son who was physically and mentally fit, but was otherwise useless. He did erratic odd jobs for a living. My aunt was married off to this person. About a month after the wedding, my grandmother said she wanted her daughter to come and stay with her for a little while, as she was missing her very much. When my aunt came back home, there was some 'good news'. She was expecting a baby! My grandmother decided that she would stay there until after the birth of the child. My aunt gave birth to a girl, and, well, she never went back to her husband's house after that. Her husband was also amenable to her staying with her mother.

The child is not epileptic. But she suffers from mental retardation. As she grew up, there was no one to look after her properly. My grandmother passed away two years after the child was born. Now, we couldn't have expected my aunt, in her situation, to give her child an upbringing at par with other children of her age.

Two years ago, when my aunt passed away, and her daughter turned sixteen, she was admitted to a special school. With no other financial support, my aunt was dependent on whatever we and my uncles gave her. This was not sufficient to live a decent life, and give her child a good education and upbringing. All the siblings helped out as much as they could, but her condition started deteriorating after the birth of her child, and became worse after my grandmother's death. She died in a very bad state.

My grandmother had thought that once her daughter was married, her husband would take care of her financial and other needs. But as it turned out, it's difficult to find a match for special children. Also, the chances that they will give birth to normal children and sustain the physical pressures of conception, pregnancy and delivery are variable, depending on the nature of the condition. It is unwise of parents to believe that marriage will ensure support for their children. On the contrary, it can complicate things.

As suggested for my aunt, the parents of special children must secure their financial future before anything else. As soon as the child is born, parents should make investments and deposits in their name, and appoint at least two trustworthy people who will keep updated about all about their finances. Some children can adapt, and learn skills that can help them earn money, whether it is painting, computers, bookkeeping, or anything they show interest in.

Our neighbour in Jabalpur, for example, has brought up her special child very intelligently. Like my aunt, her daughter, as I have mentioned above, suffered from epilepsy. When we moved in, I was still in school. I remember the first time I saw the woman with the disorder. She was strolling with her mother one evening. She immediately reminded me of my aunt.

But, unlike my aunt, she was adequately mobile. I would see her going out with a bag quite often. She would stroll around the compound with her mother every evening. If you passed by, she would exchange greetings at the very least, if not a full conversation. Her gait was staggered, but she walked. Her speech was sluggish, but she had a lot to say. She had an opinion about lots of social developments, like the fact that her maid's children were going to English-medium schools, or that elderly parents were being left to live alone as their children ventured out to pursue their professional dreams. She was a volunteer with one of Mother Teresa's orphanages in Jabalpur. Initially, her independence, considering her disorder, surprised me. But nonetheless, I appreciated it.

All the credit goes to her mother. She had planned her daughter's future really well. Beginning with daily money management, she had all the finances planned for her daughter. She took her along to the market, so that she knew how to interact and buy things herself. She involved her in social activities and interactions with the neighbours. Once, when my mother had had an eye surgery, we were not able to find a particular medicine in any of the chemists nearby. The daughter, who had epilepsy, immediately said that she knew a chemist who always had everything in stock. She asked for the prescription and said she would get the medicine for my mother. She rejected my offer to accompany her, saying that I should not leave my mother alone at home in case she needed something. And that evening, she brought over the medicine.

Her mother had made her independent enough to handle daily monetary transactions. She used to say that she did not want her daughter to be dependent on her two brothers. She had prepared her daughter to lead an independent life after her mother was not around. Unfortunately, the daughter never had to live without her mother. She passed away last year, leaving her mother free of worry about her special daughter's life after her own death.

Another mother who lived down the lane from our bungalow worked out her special son's financial future equally intelligently. Her younger son suffers from mental retardation. Her older son would occasionally come to our house to play with my brother when they were growing up. Being a junior official in a government department, their father did not have enough money to really secure his children's financial futures. Their mother would sometimes tell my mother all about her domestic issues. Once, she told her that she had made some very small investments for her younger son with the money that her father sent her as a gift for some festival or other. But she said these would never be enough to support her son for his entire life. She wanted to ensure a constant income for him, which would be adequate for his material needs.

To begin with, she said, she had asked her husband to teach their son how to frame photos, which was what the husband did to earn some extra money aside from his regular job. Their son had displayed some interest in this, and would voluntarily offer assistance when his father was working. The son is now twenty-one years old and has learnt typing. His older brother has been teaching him how to use the computer as well. Once he learns how to operate a computer, the whole world will open up for him. The family is now working towards getting him a job. This is wisdom well-applied. The mother was thoughtful and intelligent in implementing a strategy to secure her child's future, and she managed it even though they were not financially affluent.

When this boy was young, his mother was worried that her elder son might not treat her younger son properly. So besides teaching her younger son to be independent, the mother also made sure that the brothers bonded like normal siblings. She made sure that her older son respected and loved his younger brother. Along with financially securing her special child's future, a mother should also see that her other children share the same rapport with their special sibling as they do with each other.

Besides the thoughtful mothers I mentioned above, I would also like to talk about a father who, after his wife's death, filled in as a mother to his three sons, one of whom suffers from a disorder. One of my first cousins is married to the eldest of these three sons.

Their mother had passed away when the three sons were still very young. Their father insisted that his special son get a good education. He also taught him to be independent, from how to pay phone and electricity bills, to buying vegetables and groceries. When writing his will, he divided his wealth equally among his three sons. He passed away four years back.

Two of the sons are engineers. The special-needs son is now thirty years old, and lives on his own, in a flat next door to the home of their father's close friend in Bilaspur.

He earns for himself by doing chores like buying groceries, and paying bills for this close friend's family.

- Teach your special children some skills that will help them earn money later in their lives.

You may feel this is not a very relevant story for this book where we are discussing a woman's role. But I must mention it here for the sake of those mothers who are rearing their special children, either single-handedly or with their partners. Fathers are most welcome to learn a few lessons too.

The biggest security for special children comes with money. If they have strong financial support, their siblings or friends will also stand by them after their parents are gone. As a mother, you play a bigger role in securing your special child's future than anyone else. You will be able to plan for their futures. If they do not have siblings, let a close friend in on their financial investments and other important details. Help them build a good circle of friends. They must have someone to hang out with or talk to after you are gone. All their friends do not need to know everything about their lives, but they must have a reasonably big group of friends to connect with emotionally.

- Money is the biggest security for special children. If they have enough money, and also know how to earn more, they will be respected by everyone around them, including their siblings.

Giving them the hope that they will be able to live their lives like other children and people around them is not a very wise thing to do. But at the same time, do not keep them from living life as they want. As a mother, you have to manage this very carefully. You have to acquaint them with their situation in a very subtle way. They must know their restrictions, but it should not come to them as a shock, which will depress them. Never make them feel sorry for themselves. And do not forget to teach them the importance of money. It is the most important lesson and the strongest support they can ever have.

THE ESPECIAL COGNITION THEORY—AND SOME THINGS TO REMEMBER

- You must know the importance of money in securing your special children's future. Everything associated with them is special. They need your special attention, and you have to understand and plan their future with special cognition.
- The most important security for a special child is financial security. Make investments in their name.
- It may be difficult for them to understand the technicalities of investing. So, don't impose it on them and make them feel bad about themselves. But definitely help them learn how to handle money. Tell them about saving. These basics are a must.
- With some disorders, it may not be possible for the affected person to understand numbers. Enlist a trusted person who can manage their finances and financial requirements without ever harming them.

- Assuming that marriage will ensure protection and security for them is foolish. One in a million may have got lucky through marriage, but that's only one in a million.
- Do not raise hopes which you know can never be fulfilled.

8

The Mother-in-Law

A mother-in-law is supposed to be like a mother to her son's wife. But mothers-in-law are the most notorious of all the new relationships a girl forms with her husband's family after getting married. Mothers-in-law are hardly ever spoken of in a positive tone. They are either ridiculed or attacked. However, a man's mother-in-law is hardly ever mentioned, and in fact, is generally praised. That's mostly because a man's mother-in-law does not live in the same house with him after he marries her daughter. Even if, in some cases, she stays with her daughter, the son-in-law is mostly out of the house for work. So there is less interaction.

But the relationship of a woman with her mother-in-law is usually strained. Generally, after marriage, the woman moves in with her husband and parents-in-law. No sooner has she moved in than we start hearing stories about arguments and fights between the mother-in-law and the daughter-in-law.

Each blames the other for this. And both are right. Both are at fault. Also, more often than not, the disagreements are related to money.

The mother-in-law is never able to approve of the daughter-in-law's spending habits. She thinks that her daughter-in-law is squandering her son's hard-earned money. She feels that she has more claim to her son's money than his wife. If the son continues to hands over all his salary or income to his parents even after marriage, without any objection from his wife, peace prevails. But such families and situations are rare. Out of all the families that I know, there is only one family which has such an arrangement, and has been living peacefully ever since the son got married fifteen years ago.

We will talk about the daughter-in-law's role in another chapter. Here, let's look at the mother-in-law's role in her rough relationship with her daughter-in-law.

One of my close friends got married a few years ago. His wife is a banker. She is very particular about household budgets and other financial transactions, and she handles them very astutely. So much so that if she feels that her mother-in-law is wrong about something, she points it out. When relatives compliment her for that, her mother-in-law retorts, 'What's so amazing about that? I used to manage all this without being a banker, and tell me if I ever went wrong. Women of my generation are better financial managers.'

- If her daughter-in-law's financial management is praised by others, the mother-in-law asserts that the women of her generation were better money managers.

Each move that the daughter-in-law makes towards taking charge, the mother-in-law takes as another blow on her hegemony. Although the daughter-in-law, being younger, is expected to make changes to suit the rules of her new family, the mother-in-law, being the elder, makes no efforts towards helping her do so. On the contrary, she actively makes it difficult for her.

Once on a Delhi-Mumbai flight, I met a lady who looked about sixty years old. She was in the seat next to mine, and from the moment that she sat down, she was continuously on the phone instructing someone about various household chores. I thought it was her maid. Her litany was cut short when she had to switch off her mobile for takeoff.

During the flight she told me that it had been over two years since her son got married, but she still has to explain things to her daughter-in-law, otherwise she does things in her own way, which does not gel with the culture of their house. For instance, she said, once her son and daughter-in-law went out shopping, and came back with six different sets of curtains. The idea was that the curtains in each room match the colour of the walls and furniture.

This went against the mother-in-law's own unwritten personal rules of spending. She said that that very day she realized that her daughter-in-law had no sense of budgeting. After that she has always accompanied her when she goes shopping. She feels that her son works so hard; why should she let anyone waste his hard-earned money? So, the mother-in-law micro-manages the family's budget, and also her daughter-in-law's budget.

At that time, I did not say anything to her. Obviously, it was not my place to comment or interfere in someone's domestic issues, so I just listened quietly.

As she talked, it reminded something one of my aunts, whose son is a rich executive, had said about her daughter-in-law; 'She is very lucky. My son slogs it out to make all this money and she squanders it with both her hands.'

Well, people spend according to the income of the family. If the husband is rich, his wife can afford to splash out. It will not hurt their finances. Unnecessary cribbing about things is an unproductive waste of time and invaluable mind space. And I would like to ask all the mothers-in-law who think like this: 'Didn't you also do this when you got married? And when your mother-in-law objected to it, didn't you also feel bad?'

Then why repeat the past? Why not learn from it, and make your daughter-in-law's life easier? I know you love your sons, but there are other ways to express your love. Why choose the most destructive one? Fathers-in-law occupy themselves with the world outside, so they do not usually indulge in this. Those who do, end up adding to the mess. Also, men have different ways of expressing their love for their children. They are generally not possessive, besides a few exceptions where fathers are possessive about their daughters, not their sons. Mothers tend to go overboard in their love and possessiveness.

They find it hard to accept that their grown-up sons need to be left alone to learn to manage their families. More often than not, they look at a daughter-in-law as someone who has entered their son's life with the aim of corroding it. They cannot imagine just leaving the couple alone in their lives together. This is very destructive, as the daughters-in-law naturally disapprove of this.

If as a mother-in-law, you micro-manage your daughter-in-law's expenditure, she will either protest or never be able to manage it on her own, which will not be good for your son's family. There is a family I know of, where the in-laws and the husband gave the newlywed bride the impression that she was not mature enough to handle the household expenses. So the mother-in-law managed the expenses. When she became too old to do it any more, and the daughter-in-law was required to step in, it was very difficult for her. She had become so dependent that she developed cold feet when she was suddenly required to take over the job. It was embarrassing, because by now her children had grown up. They (and their friends) thought of her as dumb! But it actually had to do a lot with living a controlled, monitored life. It was like suddenly being set free in the jungle and asked to find your own food.

Such cases are rare. Mostly, women who have controlling mothers-in-law protest. To begin with, it's a silent protest. This usually does not work, and the protest gets louder. I don't need to give real-life examples to prove this. Such situations are all around us, in almost every house where the newlyweds live under the same roof as the husband's mother.

Recently, a friend told me about her husband's brother's wife, who does not talk to anyone in her in-laws' family, although she lives with her parents-in-law. The problem is that the mother-in-law wants to keep a check on how her daughter-in-law uses her husband's money. She also makes a fuss about her share of her son's salary being reduced after marriage. The son says that now the same amount must stretch to tend to his own family as well. He gives some money to his mother and wife for their respective personal expenses, some to his wife for household expenses, and yet another chunk he keeps for his personal expenses and investments.

He says the money is being utilized for the right purposes. He thinks now his mother should relax, while he and his wife do the legwork of managing the household. But that's not enough to make his mother happy. If her daughter-in-law buys spices of an expensive brand, she objects to it. She tells her that when she was young, they used to grind spices at home, which cost much less. This is highly impractical, considering today's lifestyles. This kind of interference has done much damage. The family has almost broken apart.

But I have also seen cases where the daughters-in-law are immature and lack the intelligence and skill to handle a household. I know a family where the daughter-in-law was stuck in the lifestyle she had before her marriage. This family was my grandmother's neighbours in Delhi. The daughter-in-law was always out with friends, and always splurging on new dresses and shoes. With such a busy schedule, she was not able to devote any time or money to household essentials. The mother-in-law would watch her, but say nothing. Some evenings when the son returned home and wanted to make himself a sandwich, he would find that there was neither cheese nor bread in the house. When the daughter-in-law would get down to cooking and discover there were no spices, she would pick up her phone and order them from the nearest grocery shop, which naturally worked out to be very expensive. Her husband used to get Sodexho coupons from office every month, which were to be used for buying groceries. But for lack of time, this economical option could never be utilized. The mother-in-law could not go out on her own as she was old, and the nearest shops were a drive away. So it was impossible for the old lady to venture out shopping on her own. The last that I heard was that the couple had moved to another house.

Such situations can be avoided. The mother-in-law, being older, must take the first step towards sorting this out. To begin with, forget that you are a mother-in-law. Try and be a mother to your daughter-in-law, but not a nagging, controlling mother. Encourage your daughter-in-law's interests. Appreciate her more often. I am sure that, at your age and with all your experience, you know how to make friends with an antagonistic person. Use those tactics here. Once your daughter-in-law is comfortable with you, she will enjoy going out shopping with you, whether it's for groceries or clothes. This will help your son's family financially, as well as help keep the peace.

- The moment the daughter-in-law joins the family, the mother-in-law must assume the role of her mother.
- Of course, the daughter-in-law should allow enough space to accommodate her mother-in-law as a mother.

On the other hand, there are families where the daughter-in-law believes she can manage the finances all on her own. She hates to have people interfere in her life. She wants to live in a nuclear set-up, so when she is forced to live with her parents-in-law, she is unhappy. In such cases, the daughter-in-law needs to mend her ways, something we have discussed in another chapter.

As for the mother-in-law in such cases, I would suggest that you detach yourself from your son's family as much as possible. I do not mean you should detach yourself emotionally, of course. But a lot of older women these days are doing productive things with their time. Keep busy. Go out more often, find a hobby or find your calling. Travel frequently. Expand your social circle. Stay occupied with some charity work or social organizations. This will help you feel important and wanted by the world outside, and you will not feel bad when your son and his wife do not involve you in their routine. It will also prevent you from imposing yourself on your children. If you are busy, you will not have the time and the mental space to nitpick and nag your daughter-in-law. And if you need help with anything, tell your son, and he will definitely get it for you. Peace will prevail.

- A mother-in-law should keep herself busy with productive activities outside the house or travelling, rather than the household's day-to-day running.

I have also seen that when outsiders give you validation, your family automatically does so as well. When your children see others approach you for advice or want to socialize with you, they will start also seeking your counsel. It's you, with all your experience and elderly wisdom, who determines how you are treated by your children and family. Gracefully hand over the reins of the house to your daughter-in-law, and distance yourself from the running of the home. Enjoy the freedom to do all that you were not able to do all these years because you were busy raising a family.

During all this, though, take a few minutes to praise your daughter-in-law. Let your praise be genuine. Make her feel comfortable. But don't overdo it to the point where you sound fake, and it becomes meaningless.

While you are making your daughter-in-law feel at home, I would suggest that under no circumstances must you reveal all your financial details to her. Keep this information to yourself until you are sure that you can trust your daughter-in-law and son.

However, as a mother-in-law you ought to be mature and fair. Keep your money and investments under your control. It's better not to reveal all your financial details to your children or their spouses unless they have proved themselves to be responsible and mature adults. Keep important information to yourself. Everybody has a close confidante in a friend or a relative; let your confidante know everything about your finances. If you have property in your name, do not will it to your children too early on. When you have to will your assets, make sure you divide them intelligently among all your children. It would be very unfair to give away all your assets to one of your children (who is usually a son) while the others get nothing just because they are well-established and you think they will not need your assistance as much.

If one of your sons has not been able to establish himself despite working hard, he may get a bigger chunk of your wealth. If all your children own their own house, except one, give that child your house in your will. Do it with the consensus of all your children. None of your children should hold a grudge against the decision. I have repeatedly referred to 'a son' who is not well-established, as opposed to a daughter, because this is how things work in our society. Between a married daughter who is not well-settled, and a son who is still struggling, the son is preferred, as it is assumed that the daughter will get her share from her in-laws.

However, be careful. Do not get carried away by one daughter-in-law who is more open about expressing her love and respect for you, while you completely ignore another shy and more submissive daughter-in-law. As an elder, you must have the acumen to judge people.

Generally, it's the mother-in-law's relationship with her daughter-in-law which is the most talked about. I think we have discussed all aspects vis-a-vis money in this relationship. A mother-in-law's relationship to her son-in-law is not talked about very much. That's because traditionally, a daughter's mother does not stay with her married daughter, so there are fewer chances of conflicts. But let us talk about a mother-in-law's relation with her son-in-law. To begin with, treat all your sons-in-law equally when it comes to financial interactions. Also, even if you disapprove of the way your daughter handles her finances, which most mothers do, do not express your concern to your son-in-law. It may not be very good for the couple's relationship in the long run.

- Don't discuss your daughter's bad money management skills with your son-in-law.

On another note, do not pamper your son-in-law too much. According to Indian tradition, the son-in-law must be showered with goodies and respected like a god. But blind devotion does no good. Draw the line according to his worth and character, and according to your net worth. An unemployed son-in-law, who whiles away his time doing nothing or trying to learn what is in his future with astrologers is worthless. A son-in-law who disrespects and ill-treats your daughter is worthless. A son-in-law who keeps your daughter from standing by you in your old age is heartless and worthless. A son-in-law who remembers you only when he has to collect gifts is worthless.

Those are a few examples of worthless sons-in-law. Let's move on to your net worth now. If you are stretching yourself beyond your means to make your son-in-law feel like a king, you are going overboard. As I have said in all the other chapters, no matter what age you are or what relationship you are in, your priority should be to keep yourself financially secure. This applies here too. Respect your son-in-law, but keep your budget under control. There is no need to overstep your budget. Pampering your son-in-law beyond a certain point is unnecessary and may prove harmful for your daughter.

- Respect your son-in-law but let your respect be a function of his worth and your net worth.

THE RADICAL ALTERATION THEORY—AND SOME THINGS TO REMEMBER

As soon as your status changes from a mother to a mother-in-law, you must know that you have the added responsibility to ensure that your son or your daughter's family is settled well. This will happen more efficiently without your voluntary involvement—as opposed to the involvement sought out by your children and their spouses. You will need to bring about some fundamental changes in your lifestyle and behaviour to help your children's families live smooth lives.

- It's best to pass on the reins to your daughter-in-law.
- If your daughter-in-law shows signs of immaturity in handling finances, don't nag her, but try to maintain a cordial relationship with her.
- Don't interfere in the management of the house, until your opinion is sought. There's so much to engage you at your age. Keep yourself busy.

- Try to keep your own finances under your control.
- As a mother-in-law to your daughter's husband, do not go overboard pampering him.

9

The Daughter-in-Law

Traditionally speaking, a daughter-in-law's status in her husband's family is only as good as the amount of material assets she brings along in the form of dowry, and the number of sons she can produce. I am close friends with a family which has three sons. The first son has a daughter and a son. The second son has two sons and the third son has four daughters. Although the mother of the three sons shows equal affection for all her grandchildren, among the daughters-in-law, the wife of the second son gets special attention. On family occasions, this daughter-in-law is more in demand than the other two, and she is totally in command all the time.

Now that the times are changing, a daughter-in-law is as good as her pay package and the number of sons she adds to the family. Daughters-in-law have a long way to go, from entering a house full of strangers to establishing themselves as daughters of the family, and according to my observations, the long way is only getting longer.

However, this long route can be shortened, with a bit of intelligence and effort on the daughter-in-law's part. All daughters-in-law are probably fuming at my statement that I have completely put everything on their shoulders, as if their in-laws have no role to play in making things work. I agree that they have to cooperate too. But you, as a daughter-in-law, are at an age when you can afford to change without negatively affecting your personality. You can even change your in-laws without making them feel bad.

- The daughter-in-law, being younger, must play a major role in helping her in-laws accommodate her.

I met a lawyer at the Bombay High Court in connection with a story I was working on in 2011. As we chatted, she told me that her cousin got had gotten married four years ago. About six months after the marriage, her sister-in-law, her husband's sister, enrolled in a fashion design course in Paris. The lawyer's cousin, who is professionally very well-established and earns much more than her husband, was asked to pay for the course from her savings. She was reluctant, as she was saving the money for investments and she was planning her future finances. But here she was being asked to give away her money for the education of a girl who was not even very serious about her career. She spoke to her parents and they advised her to give in, as 'these small things should not mar the marriage'. So she did.

Now, four years later, this woman has not yet been able to save an amount equal to what she spent on educating her sister-in-law, and which she had actually wanted to invest in property and stocks. By the way, her sister-in-law left the fashion design course midway to got married. But she never complained. Her marriage is intact, and she is happy. Her in-laws are happy. Her husband is happy. Her parents are happy. And I am confused. My lawyer friend is all praise for her cousin who 'made a big sacrifice to keep her marriage rolling'.

What concerns me is the attitude of all the players in this reality show. The rich in-laws who own properties in various expensive locations in Mumbai, and have an investment banker for a son, did not pay for their daughter's education. Why? The daughter-in-law emptied her humble coffers to pay for their daughter's future. If they didn't have the heart to spend on their own daughter's needs, would they come forward if there was an emergency where their daughter-in-law required financial help? I don't think so. What will the daughter-in-law do then? She slogged to make her future secure, but she might still find herself stranded. Also, such a situation renders her dependent on other people, even though she had taken good care to make herself independent.

In such situations, if the daughter-in-law does not have enough money, or if she is not working, she is told to ask her parents for financial help. Her parents will oblige. But this can go awry at times, if the in-laws start demanding money too frequently from their daughter-in-law's parents. In many cases, the daughter-in-law's parents report this as a case of dowry-related harassment, and sue the girl's in-laws under the dowry prohibition laws. Things may get out of hand as more relatives and friends get involved. Everybody will have a view and, mind you, excepting a couple of them, no one will give you any advice which will help bring your family together. Some of them will pitch in for entertainment, and in doing so, give you suggestions that will only drive you closer towards a split.

But you, as a daughter-in-law, can avoid all this trouble without compromising your financial security or your marriage. For this, it's important that you understand your in-laws' disposition regarding money. This generally happens only after you start living with them after you are married. Sometimes their intentions become clear before marriage, when they talk about dowry and wedding gifts. If you know their views before marriage, you have the option of calling off the wedding if they seem overly interested in money or anything material. But if this is revealed after marriage, which is more likely, then you have only one choice, and that is to work things out intelligently, without hurting your new relatives' sentiments, and without letting your finances go haywire.

- A daughter-in-law must understand her husband's and her in-laws' attitudes towards money, and work things out without hurting either their sentiments or her finances.

If you are in a situation like the lawyer's cousin in the example above, you can suggest to your in-laws some alternate ways to fund their children's education, rather than having to proffer your own money. You may broach the idea of a student loan, or suggest that the family pool its resources. You can tell them how much you can contribute personally; this contribution from you should be from the surplus that you have after considering your financial plans. So, even if you are not able to extend any financial assistance, you are not leaving your new family in the lurch. You are helping them out with ideas and suggestions; you can even offer to help them with the paperwork if they agree to any of your suggestions.

Some may think that this will make women selfish when it comes to dealing with their in-laws. It will not. This will ensure that even if you don't have money, you are there to help them. As I mentioned above, you can suggest ways to source funds, and make yourself available for any other sort of help they may need.

Also, if you do have a lot of money and your in-laws request financial help, you can lend them some money. But you must have enough, so that this lending does not leave you stranded later on, when you need money for yourself, your children or your husband.

Yet, I strongly believe that rather than giving people money, a better way to help them is to show them the ways in which they can make money for themselves. This reminds me of a famous Stephen Covey quote: 'Give a man a fish and you feed him for a day; teach him to fish and you feed him for a lifetime.'

On a spiritual note, it is believed that if you are hungry and you have one fish, but another hungry person approaches you, you should give him your fish—God will reward you with a thousand more. In other words, if you give everything that you have away to a needy person, God will replenish your emptied coffers for you.

Fair enough. When a hungry person approaches me, I will give him the fish that I have, no matter how hungry I am; along with that, I will also teach him how to fish. My idea behind giving him the fish first is that he should survive through the fishing tutorials at least!

You may think that this contradicts my previous statement where I tell the daughter-in-law not to give away her money and instead show her in-laws alternate solutions. But it is not.

Here I am talking about a needy, hungry person. But in the example above, where the daughter-in-law funded her sister-in-law's education, she was not giving her money to any needy, hungry people. Her parents-in-law were fully capable of paying for their children's education; even if they did not have the finances to hand, they could easily have got a loan from the bank. They could never be classified as 'needy'. You must understand this difference.

Recently, I met a young guy who had literally given away all his earnings to his various friends. When he needed money, he had to fall back on his family or other friends. The friends to whom he had been lending money were from rich families. When this young man's mother objected to his anti-Robin Hood ways, he curtly told her, 'You always preach to the world that you must help those in need. But now when I am doing it, you object!' Well, of course, sons of rich businessmen, who cannot frequently ask their parents for money, are 'needy'! Do not confuse 'greedy' with 'needy'.

- If your in-laws are financially capable of paying for an emergency that they are asking you to pay for, politely refuse and offer them an alternative solution.

I also suggest that while dating or when they are getting married, women should not reveal all the details about their financial investments and savings to their partner's family. You may reveal this information a few years after your marriage, when you know your husband and your in-laws better, and also know that they will not misuse this information. Do it when you are comfortable. If you are even slightly doubtful, don't. But here again, I may be cornered by some people saying that this may amount to lying to your husband.

- A daughter-in-law must not reveal the details of her finances to her husband or in-laws unless she knows them really well and knows that they will not misuse the information.

Conventionally, it's believed that keeping any information secret from your husband is akin to cheating. Well, I am not quite a supporter of this belief when it comes to professional and financial details. If you are investing money from your individual account, and not from the joint account that you have with your husband, then it is not mandatory for you to reveal all details to your husband. What you do with the money in your individual account is no concern of your husband or your in-laws. If you think this is mean, I must correct you. You are not being mean to anyone. You are only securing your future with your own money. You are doing this because you are slogging day and night to make your life comfortable. You deserve it. You wouldn't want someone to swoop in one day and take away your life savings, even as you look on helplessly.

So, get to know your new family well before you reveal all your secrets to them. Judge them on how they treat money generally, how they handle the family's money matters, and how they treat other people's money.

If you say that in the case of the lawyer's cousin, the in-laws regarded their daughter-in-law's money as their own, and that is why they asked her to spend it on their daughter's education, I would beg to disagree. These days there are hardly any parents who have not saved money for their children's higher education. In the above example, their daughter had just completed high school and had expressed her desire to study abroad. Like any self-respecting human being, her parents should have either told her that they could not afford to pay for her education abroad and that she could enrol in a similar course at a good college in India, or, if she insisted on going to Paris, they should have taken an education loan.

Besides, I refuse to believe that they did not know about their daughter's temperament. In all likelihood, they knew quite well that she was not very serious about her studies, and might not even complete the course. It was a gamble for them to invest in her education abroad. So they asked their daughter-in-law to fund it. When people treat your money as their own, they are very careful about using it. It's like how people treat public property and private property. They are extremely careful about their own house and possessions. But when it comes to public property, no one can beat them in carelessness.

But even as you decide to follow the above advice, be careful that you don't put your in-laws' backs up. You must manage it very subtly, in such a way that their interests are looked after, even as your financial future remains secure. When you are reacting to such situations, remember that you have to give suggestions that will bring your family closer together rather than split it up. Do not say things like 'I can't help. I am not earning so much as to adopt the whole world.' Instead, say, 'I have a better idea!' Give them a list of alternatives. Tell them how much you can offer, and offer just as much as you can without disturbing your own finances. You have to keep your family intact. Deal with your in-laws as you would with your own family. But make sure that you are not left stranded in an emergency.

- When a daughter-in-law tries sorting out financial issues at her husband's family's home, she must do it with the intention of keeping the family intact rather than breaking it up.

Besides this, another issue that most daughters-in-law face is their mother-in-law objecting to their spending. Even if the daughter-in-law is employed, and spending her own money, her mother-in-law nags. And even if she shops for the family from the joint account she holds with her husband, her mother-in-law nags. For home-bound daughters-in-law, the issue can get even more serious, because their mothers-in-law often think that their sons' hard-earned money is being wasted. The best way to handle this is to buy a little something for your mother-in-law every time you go shopping. But, chances are she may object to that too. Then the only solution is to talk to her. When you put up those curtains she objected to, tell her how beautiful they look and how people are admiring them. Take her out shopping with you. Make friends with her. You may not like whatever she says. She may be on a completely different wavelength. But think of the boring friends you have. We all hate so many little things about our friends, but we are still friends. Look at your mother-in-law as a friend who just happens to have the annoying habit of being an old-fashioned nag. Pamper her. She will like it. You will like it too.

- The only way for a daughter-in-law to handle a nagging mother-in-law is to make friends with her. Take her out shopping. She should know that you are spending money only to make your shared home look better.

Home-bound daughters-in-law have some other issues related to money. I have come across a lot of families where the husband hands over money to his parents or mother every month for household expenses, but his wife is not able to accept this arrangement. She wants to be in charge of the house. But it is not easy for the husband to change the set-up suddenly. When she talks about it with her husband, he is not able to do much about it, as it is his mother on the other side. If the mother-in-law hands over the household duties to her daughter-in-law, there is no problem. But if the mother-in-law takes any interference as a slight to herself, it can be the beginning of a long domestic battle.

When families break up because of such issues, both the mother-in-law and daughter-in-law are to be equally blamed. As they say, it needs two to tango. When I lived in Delhi for a couple of years, there was an old couple who lived in my building. I often saw them sitting alone on the common building lawns at all times of the day. I would feel sad that they were all alone at this age, with no company and no one to talk to. Later, I discovered that their son lives in another block in the same housing complex, with his working wife and their six-year-old daughter.

The story goes that the son and his wife lived with his parents for four years after getting married. The last six months of these four years were full of loud quarrels between the daughter-in-law and mother-in-law. They fought because the mother-in-law was a nag, the daughter-in-law wanted privacy, the mother-in-law refused to cook, and the daughter-in-law couldn't cook because she was working. And they fought because the daughter-in-law felt that her husband was giving too much money to his parents and in the course of it, her dreams, his desires and their daughter's needs were being put on hold. Cheesed off with the recurring arguments, the husband decided to move out along with his family.

Whatever emotional setback the adults went through during this time, it had an adverse effect on their daughter. She is six years old now and every day the parents of other children in the neighbourhood complain that she is spoilt and is spoiling their children as well. She does not go to her grandparents' house after school, because she has seen them fighting with her mother.

Joint families are still very popular in our society, in smaller cities as well as in metropolitan areas. I know of many young couples who live with their parents in both Delhi and Mumbai. Of course, in non-metropolitan cities, you are likely to bump into joint families more frequently. I have noticed that in some joint families, even if the husband hands over an equal amount of money to his parents and his wife, there is disagreement over who should spend on household expenses. The wife wants to spend all the money on herself and her children. This makes the mother-in-law crib, and then in protest, she does not shell out a penny either.

However, now we live in times where many parents in urban set-ups are independent even after retirement. They don't usually fall back on their children for financial help, regardless of whether it's a son or daughter. Also, most wives are employed and earning now. So these conflicts are not very frequent these days. But there is still a reasonably large number of old parents who depend on their children for money.

Recently, one of my friends got married. There is a tradition that after the wedding, the couple and their families are invited to lunch or dinner by their close relatives. After the meal, the hosts give some gifts or money to the newlyweds as a token of affection. On one such occasion, when the couple came home, the wife went straight upstairs with all the presents. Her husband went right after her, and brought her back, explaining that these should be handed over to his grandmother, as the oldest in the family. It was smart on the part of my friend to explain the set-up of the house to his wife, and it was equally intelligent on his wife's part to have understood the arrangement, and agreeing to do as he asked, instead of keeping all the presents and arguing that the grandmother had no need of money at her age.

A daughter-in-law would do well by not objecting to her husband handing over his salary or a part of it to his parents. If there is a grandparent in the house, she must give them due respect in terms of money too.

Another example in my family is that of the wife of one of my first cousins. My cousin is an only child. After finishing his studies, he joined the family business. He has always lived with his parents, even after getting married. My aunt and uncle were aggressive and controlling parents. The family business was run by my uncle and my cousin, and the income went to the parents. My cousin would get some money, which he would spend on his wife and himself. This continued for about ten years after his marriage, when my uncle decide to divide up the income from the business. It was then that my cousin started earning a good salary from their business. But during those ten years of 'pocket money', there were never any complaints from my cousin's wife about why they got only a token amount from his parents when her husband worked so hard. It's been fourteen years now, and recently, my cousin has set up a gym, the income from which goes to him, without any interference from his parents.

Initially, my cousin's wife did have adjustment issues. But

she handled it very smartly. She never cribbed during the initial years, and didn't let the fact that her husband had to ask for money from his parents when his token 'pocket money' had run out, affect her ego. The result of this was that her mother-in-law, my aunt, was very considerate to her daughter-in-law. She really cared about what she liked and disliked, and would always bring her back something when she went out on her own.

The daughter-in-law did the same. She formed a bond with her parents-in-law, and treated her husband's extended family like her own. When we would visit, she would make us feel so comfortable that we immediately felt at home. She immediately became a part of our family. Credit should go to the parents-in-law as well, but it was the daughter-in-law who had come to a new home, to live surrounded by new people. She made significant changes in her lifestyle to gel with the new family, and her parents-in-law reacted positively. Such families are few and far between these days. Shouldn't I be proud that they are part of my extended family?

Before his marriage, my father used to give all his monthly salary to his mother, to use as she saw fit. This continued even after he got married. A couple of years after his marriage, when he got promoted and became eligible for a government-allotted house, he moved in along with my mother and me. At that time, two of my uncles had recently gotten married, and the old ancestral house was becoming too cramped for the expanding family. When my parents moved to an independent set-up, my mother started handling my father's salary, although they continued to contribute some part of it to my grandparents. Later, my father bought his parents a sprawling plot in a posh colony in Jabalpur.

The house was built with some contribution from my grandfather. The whole joint family moved in while we continued living in government accommodation. My mother never objected to my father giving money to his parents. In fact my mother was one up among all her sisters-in-law when it came to giving her in-laws gifts, and she still is. Even after my father's death, she is particular about her interaction with her in-laws, especially my father's sisters and their children. Whether it's festivals, weddings, or even deaths, she never ignores her role as the oldest daughter-in-law of the family.

Even as I write this, she has gone to Delhi to meet my father's sister for a couple of days. Last month, my aunt lost her husband to chronic illness. She is now on her way back home to Chhindwara after completing her husband's last rites on the banks of the Ganga in Haridwar. The tradition is that a widowed daughter's family present her with clothes after her husband's death. My mother could not make it to Chhindwara when she heard the news, so she is meeting my aunt in Delhi, along with clothes for her and her two children, a bagful of other gifts and also some money.

Sometimes I get upset with my mother for being so over-generous, but she says this is a token of affection and regard for the daughters of a family that is her family as well. She says that she is doing what my father would have done had he been around. That shuts me up right away. Deep down, I appreciate what she is doing. Unfortunately, it's that tainted thing called 'money' which keeps relations intact, but as long as it keeps relationships alive, nothing else matters. Money helps keep relationships going. If you have enough money, never refrain from giving gifts generously to your in-laws. As long as you don't overstep your budget.

As a daughter-in-law, you play a very important role in maintaining peace and love in the family. You are young and belong to a generation which is more flexible. You are better equipped to handle things intelligently. The best way to strike a positive chord with your in-laws, especially your mother-in-law, is to make friends with her. This is what we call the Mystique Bond Theory.

THE MYSTIQUE BOND THEORY—AND SOME THINGS TO REMEMBER

This theory deals with striking a positive, friendly chord with your in-laws, especially your mother-in-law. I call it 'mystique' because this sort of bond is very difficult to establish; but once established, its aura is unmatched. This bond is one of the most complex and the most fascinating ones in our lives. And it's the daughter-in-law who will have to make the most effort to build it.

- If your in-laws ask for financial help, and you cannot oblige without hurting your own financial security, offer help by advising them about alternate means.

- Reveal your personal financial details to your husband and in-laws only after you have known them for a few years after marriage.
- If you have known your husband long enough before marriage, then you can tell him about your financial status before marriage. He should know what you are capable of. But still keep some crucial personal financial information to yourself.
- If your mother-in-law objects to your way of handling the household budget, try having a dialogue with her.
- If your mother-in-law interferes with the way you are bringing up your children, you must again have a conversation with her. She must know that times have changed, and the child-rearing methods of her day cannot be applied today.
- If your mother-in-law is keen to handle the household budget, and your husband gives her the money for the family expenses every month, stay calm. Let her handle it, but stay by her side to assist her if she needs your help.
- If your husband passes away, you must continue interacting with your in-laws. Relationships matter. Keep them intact. And the best way to keep them going is with money. But, yes, don't overstep your budget.

10

The Friend

I have read that you can choose your friends but not your family. But after a point, this rule becomes redundant. You cannot afford to go around rejecting friends just because you have the liberty to choose new ones. And you cannot do without your friends, since they are the ones with whom you can share things you sometimes cannot tell your parents or even your siblings.

I have seen a lot of friendships break up because of money. I know a rich businessman's twenty-something son who was always surrounded by friends. Then the news broke that his father had donated all his wealth to an orphanage, and the son had inherited nothing. His girlfriend was the first to leave him, followed by his other friends. Later, when the son came into some money, his ex-girlfriend wanted to come back to him. But he had already found his true love in his days of poverty.

I have seen friends abandon each other because one or the other would never chip in to pay a bill. Others have parted ways because one friend overused another's credit card. Some other guy stole their friend's card or money. When it comes to women, specifically, they tend to get very micro-managerial. In an all-woman group, money is a very sensitive subject. Women keep a close watch on who is spending how much, and they are quick to point out even the slightest imbalance.

I have come across people who get home after a holiday, and immediately start calculating the expenses. When they discover that they spent more than the other family member or friend, their immediate reaction is: 'Be careful the next time you go out with this person. They're very smart; they know how to make others spend their money and hold back themselves.'

TRAVELLING WITH WOMEN

I have a friend who has learnt her money lessons. Anoushqa is addicted to travelling. She travels so frequently that I often forget which city she actually lives in. And she never travels alone. It's always with at least three friends at a time. I once asked her how she was able to find people to travel with her each time. She said the first and the most important thing she does is declare that the expenses will not be combined. Common expenses like the car journey, etc., would be equally shared among all the travellers in the group, but after that, each person would be responsible for their own expenditures. Anoushqa said that she had noticed early on that money was the most important aspect of a holiday, and if not tackled properly, it could ruin the trip.

I have noticed that men are not as picky about these things. When I hang out with my male friends, I have noticed there is absolutely no fuss about expenses. Not that they keep track of every little thing. Each one just offers to pay the bill, in turn. All in all, money never mars their outings. When I go out with my brother and our common friends or cousins, it's always me and my female cousins or friends who keep track of how much is being spent. The men are largely not fussy. It's understood among them that they are going Dutch. If everybody does not have the cash at one particular outing, then whoever does pays, and someone else picks up the cheque the next time. This is the unspoken arrangement. But among women, it has to be spoken.

Then there's that one friend who always gets a phone call right when it's time to pay the bill for a group dinner or outing. Suddenly her phone signal will falter and she will have to excuse herself and go outside to be able to hear the caller. This call lasts until the monetary rituals are performed, and all the others come out to leave. The only way to tackle such pals is to declare right at the beginning that you are going Dutch. They might make the excuse of having forgotten their wallet. Tell them politely that they can pay the next time. This is just to make sure that they do not develop selective amnesia and forget their wallet the next time.

THE RICH FRIEND

If you have a friend who is better off than you, she may be happy to spend her money on you and treat you to expensive meals. Although this comes out of her goodwill, you must draw the line somewhere, and sooner rather than later. Even if your friend doesn't feel it herself, she may be made to feel by others around her that you are 'using' her to have a good time. She may start to think that you are friends with her just because of her money. That will, of course, scar the friendship, and it will also hurt your self-esteem. So even if your friend is richer than you are, you must still contribute if you want to keep your friendship going strong.

- If you have a rich friend, she should not *always* foot the bill. Go Dutch!

HANGING OUT WITH A COUPLE

When you go out with a friend and her boyfriend, chances are that the boyfriend, out of chivalry, will not let the women pay. I have gone out with couples quite a few times. We would eat snacks at various places, and I would foot the bill at half the places, while my friend's boyfriend treated us at the others.

- If you are going out with a couple, the man should not pay for you. Either split expenses, or be the host.

It's not just the group's expenses; when it comes to borrowing and lending, women tend to be quite finicky.

Long ago, I had a flatmate who never bought her own kitchen utensils or spices or even vegetables. Whenever she was cooking, she went to the other three flatmates, including me, asking for this and that. After this happened a couple of times, she became the topic of gossip in the flat. Someone suggested that the next time she came asking for something, nobody should oblige her; and no one did, after this diktat. This was a case of excessive borrowing.

BORROWING AND LENDING

This is how it works among women: when a woman lends a friend money, it lingers on her mind till that person returns the money. She will not forget it. If the money does not come back within a reasonable period of time, there's severe heartburn. After waiting for a while, she may even make a rude phone call asking point-blank for the money. I have never really borrowed money, not even from my family. But once I was stuck because of a debit card malfunction. We had a work event the next day and I had to buy some supplies. The wholesaler I was buying everything from didn't accept cards, so I had to make the payment in cash. When I went to withdraw money, the ATM showed that there was a problem with the card, and hence no money could be withdrawn. I tried at two other ATMs close by. No luck! It was eight o'clock in the morning and no banks were open yet, so I couldn't withdraw any money directly either.

Stranded, I called a very close friend who lived nearby, and asked if she could help with Rs 3,000. She did. I told her that I would return the money the day after the next. Our event finished the next afternoon, and when I left work, the first thing I did was go to the bank and sort out the problem with my ATM card, then withdraw the money I owed my friend. She was going to get home late that night, so I thought I'd call her around nine o'clock the next morning before she left for work, and give her the money. But the next morning, at around seven o' clock, while I was still fast asleep, I got a phone call from my friend, asking if I could come and give her the money right then! I thought it a little weird, not to mention rude. But anyway, neither of us dwelt on the issue, and we are still friends.

This is the best way to handle sticky situations when it comes to money, because if money problems drag on, they can lead to a very unpleasant atmosphere among friends. If things get even more difficult, the only thing you can do is avoid asking for monetary help from that particular friend in the future. As for me, I am totally against borrowing. However, if you must borrow, make sure you return the money by the date agreed upon. If you are the lender, give your friend a grace period of at least a day before you remind them. Women are generally very impatient money-lenders, so avoid badgering your friends if you want to maintain the friendship.

REVEALING YOUR FINANCIAL DETAILS

Another thing that you must be careful about with friends is revealing your financial details. Refrain from telling even your closest friends the details of your cards, accounts, bank balances and investments. I have heard of quite a few cases of friends being robbed when they live in shared accommodation. Their cards go missing and are swiped for huge amounts before the owner finds out. Finally, it is revealed that it was a close friend who stole the card.

I had a friend who never kept her financial details secret from her friends. One day she lost her debit card in the flat she shared with five other girls. She was very friendly with three of the girls, who knew everything about her cards and bank balances. She blamed all of them for the lost card, reasoning that only they could have used the card. This scarred her relationship with them for good. About a week later, when she was spring cleaning, she found the card lying under her bed. It seemed that what had happened was that the card had been in her pocket, and when she lay down on the bed, it slipped out and made its way into the gap between the wall and the bed. She found her card but lost her friends.

The key is to keep your refrigerator in order rather than blame the world for things going stale later on. Keep your financial details strictly to yourself, and keep your financial interactions with friends organized and open. This will help avoid unnecessary blame and mistrust later on. Friends are important, and only a few of us have really good ones. If you have good friends, do not let money become a spoilsport. Keep watch!

THE CORDIALITY CONTINUUM THEORY—AND SOME THINGS TO REMEMBER

Even as money plays a pivotal role in friendships, you must be careful about where it gets too problematic to handle. Your aim should be to protect your friendship from being affected by the vagaries of materialism.

- When you go out with friends or go on holiday as a group, go Dutch. Declare this beforehand to avoid problems later on.
- Refrain from lending or borrowing, unless you are pushed to the wall. If you must borrow, return the money at the appointed date or even before that. If you lend, don't be rude and start reminding the borrower about returning it before the agreed-upon date.
- If you have a rich friend, refrain from letting her always pay for you. Go Dutch, just as you do with your other friends.
- Do not reveal your financial details even to your closest friends. This will go a long way towards avoiding bad blood in your friendship.

11

The Single Woman

Until only a few years ago, a single woman in India was seen as the devil's handiwork. She was often regarded with scorn and suspicion. Single women had to justify why they had chosen to live the way they had, and those who were rendered single by chance were forced by their relatives and friends to remarry. As a result of this mentality, women would try to 'adjust' to circumstances like a difficult marriage rather than walk out on their husbands. Others, who would have preferred to stay single, gave in to social pressure and unwillingly tied the knot.

Now we have moved forward a little. Women are choosing to remain unmarried for the simple reason that they want to live life on their own terms. They are talking to their parents about their preferences, rather than quietly accepting the dictates of fate. In many cases, their parents are supportive. They expect that their daughters professionally establish themselves before getting married. In cases where the parents insist on marriage against their daughter's wishes, the daughters usually rebel. And, yes, I must make it clear that all these women who protest marriage or early marriage are working women.

Non-working women cannot afford to do this, as they are financially dependent on their families, and their parents worry that they will not be able to provide for their daughters forever. So they will need a husband to support them. This reason is never directly stated. That's because money is an emotional topic. People generally avoid talking about it lest it make them look greedy or poor.

A change is occurring. But it's coming from women, who are bringing about change by being the change. But society as a whole is still a long way from accepting the new way of life.

Sometime in May 2012, an uncle of mine asked my cousin (in my absence), 'You are getting old. Don't you plan to get married, or are you planning to follow in the footsteps of Shruti?' This is when I haven't yet stated that I plan to remain unmarried forever. And this is just one of the many family conversations that revolve around my singledom.

Other people who know about my marital status, and are meeting me for the first time, greet me with an 'Oh!' which, they tell me later, is because they are surprised to see me as I am. They come expecting to meet some 'poor, helpless loser', bogged down by the failure to find a man for herself. They also usually tell me that they had prepared a speech advising me 'to be brave and not worry'.

At a recent family gathering, an aunt wanted to know all

about my business. I gave her the lowdown. Her last question was whether I had business partners. I told her I did not. Her response (with a huge friendly grin) was: 'That's okay. But you must get a life partner now.'

However, I also know a lot of other people, especially people my age and younger, who greet me with, 'Oh, wow! Single is hot!' Others of my parents' generation have told me, 'Marriage can wait. Work can't. It's really difficult for women to pursue high-intensity careers alongside the domestic responsibilities that come with marriage. Good luck!'

Society is still far away from the day when a woman's single status is accepted as just another relationship status. Single women have to don that no-nonsense garb in offices, professional gatherings, even family gatherings, wherever they go, to discourage unnecessary advances from men who are attuned to thinking that 'single' means 'available' by default. And let me point out here that most men looking for single women's company are married men.

My cousin, who lives in the US, is very good friends with a couple who got married after having been together for a long time. One weekend, a year after their marriage, when the wife had come to India to visit her parents, the husband called up my cousin, who is single, and suggested an evening out. This was not at all strange, since they were good friends. However, he added, that after dinner at their favourite spot they could go back to his place and have some fun, as his wife was not around. My cousin still didn't sense anything weird about this. She asked what sort of 'fun' he was planning. He said, 'What sort of fun can two hot people have? And you are single, that makes you doubly hot.' My cousin, who was shocked and angry, reminded him that he had a wife. He replied, 'But there's something about single women.'

When an unmarried woman wants to do something which is unacceptable to conservative society, she is told she can do whatever she likes after she is married. My friend, who has lived in Boston for eight years, recently returned to Delhi to live with her parents. One day when she was planning to come home fairly late at night, her mother told her, 'Wait till you are married. You can do all this then.'

Women must make themselves emotionally strong and not react to comments about their single status. And this emotional strength will come from financial strength. With money comes power, because with money comes independence. And there is no power bigger than independence.

Single women must have a concrete financial plan in place, which they must adhere to strictly. This is my advice for all women, single or married, but for single women, this is even more essential.

In 2009, on a work trip to Goa, during my daily run on the beach, I encountered a woman who was out on her morning walk. We crossed each other a couple of times, and on our third encounter, we exchanged greetings and fell into conversation. We decided to continue our chat over dinner that evening. When we met, we discovered a shared love of Goan fish curry (I was a non-vegetarian back then), and then the conversation shifted to more personal subjects.

This woman was a civil servant in the IAS's Punjab cadre, and she had chosen Goa as her last posting, as she had always wanted to spend her retired life in Goa. She was forty-nine years old, and had applied for voluntary retirement, which was in six months' time. She told me she was single by choice. Then the conversation shifted to living in Goa. She told me she had bought a flat in Palolem, and would be moving in after her retirement. At the moment, she lived in a government bungalow. She had decided very early in her life that she would settle in Goa, and had her retirement planned accordingly. This was very impressive.

Most single women manage their finances pretty well, although some live hand-to-mouth till very late in life. Then they realize that time is running out and they need to do something about it. That's fine. Start when you realize this for yourself. But do not procrastinate after you have understood the significance of financial independence.

Sometime in the summer of 2010, I was interviewing a socialite and theatre actor for my magazine *MoneyQuin*. One of my questions concerned investments. The actor said that she did not believe in saving and investing. When she gets an assignment, she pays her bills. She said she had given standing instructions to everybody around her that she does not want to be resuscitated in case of an emergency, and that she never wants artificial tubes in her body keeping her alive. She has lived a good life and she wants to die naturally.

Well, I really like her spirit. But unfortunately, most of us don't think of death in quite that spirit. We want to live forever, and when the time comes, the only thing that can buy us life is money, along with, of course, prayers. So single women have to be adequately armed with money at all times.

- Keep yourself financially ready for any emergency. Not all women have generous siblings and parents.

Yet another reason why single women have to be extra careful about being financially strong is because they often meet men who are eager to 'support' them. But of course they want something in return. Beware! Unless you think you will never regret your decision, despite all the humiliation it brings. Nothing stays behind closed doors for long. Eventually the world will find out about your noble and not-so-noble deeds. I recommend that you stay away from such 'liaisons-for-money' arrangements, because very few women have been able to take the consequences.

Such relationships usually leave women unhappy in the long run, because most of these relationships tend to be between married men and single women. Even if the men are unmarried, they look at the relationship as a business deal where they give money and receive pleasure. But finally, the woman ends up shattered, while the man turns to another bed mate. Some women, like men, also end up with another partner. But in such relationships, if someone is going to end up a wreck, it's invariably the woman.

When it comes to independent single women, I must mention my schoolteacher, Ms Jenny M. Vyse, whom I look up to immensely. She is single and I admire her lifestyle. She has always kept herself busy with numerous social activities besides her routine office work. After she retired in early

2011, she has been busy exploring new career opportunities. She does not want to go back to teaching. Although she splurges and lives a good, lavish life, she has dabbled in investing and insurance.

Women, who are rendered suddenly single, that is, by divorce or by the death of their husband, are usually not prepared to handle being single. Even working women are sometimes not ready to handle sudden, imposed singledom. That is why I have stressed elsewhere in this book that even if you are married, you must keep yourself updated about how your salary is being invested.

Whether you are single by choice or by chance, you should be financially prepared for the present as much as for the future. Under no circumstances should you find yourself forced to pull out your begging bowl—er, I mean, resort to borrowing. That's why single women inevitably have to be professionals. If you are single because of a tragedy like divorce or the death of your husband, find a job which will bring you some income. If you are too old for a job, make sure you go all out to understand your husband's investments to ensure your financial security. If your husband has left you some property, don't make the mistake of transferring it to your children.

If there is a pension coming to you, regard it as your salary and use it intelligently. For women who are rendered single because of their husband's sudden demise, it can be very difficult to learn something technical all of a sudden. That's why I always stress the need for women, whether housewives or professionals, to keep themselves abreast of financial terms and procedures, even if their husbands actually do the investments.

Use your time to put the pension and other income from various investments to proper productive use. Do not shy away from investments now even if you never bothered about them when your partner was alive. This goes for working women as well. I have come across quite a few working women who, when their husbands passed away, were left clueless about their investments. Interestingly, these women never wanted to go solo on investments, even after being left in the lurch.

When I visited my hometown Jabalpur three years ago, one of my schoolteachers called me and asked me to come and see her. Her brother had passed away a few days ago, and her widowed sister-in-law, who is a schoolteacher in Mumbai, had come to visit her. I was told that she needed some help with her personal finances. I assumed she wanted to invest in something. But actually, she was bewildered by all the phone calls and visits from broking houses after her husband passed away. She told me she did not understand a word of what was being said to her, but she did not want to give that away to the brokers' agents who were visiting her.

I helped her understand the details of her husband's investments. Afterwards, she said that she would be redeeming all the investments. She said, 'I will not be able to handle all this financial planning and all.' I offered to help her out, but she declined. Well, that is her choice. As long as she has her job, it's fine. But I wondered what would happen to her after her retirement. She doesn't even have a house of her own. If she expects to rely on her son, I would say that's not a very wise idea.

However, I have also met a suddenly single woman who is a Mumbai-based socialite. She separated from her husband over a decade ago. She told me, 'I do not believe in investing. I have enough savings to manage an emergency.' Well, she can afford to do this because, even at sixty, she is still working and earning. But I asked her what would happen in a situation where the expenses of the emergency exceeded her savings. She ended the discussion with a spiritual reply, 'When we are in trouble, if help has to come, it comes from somewhere.'

I am not quite in agreement with this belief. We cannot just expect to be taken care of in trouble. On the contrary, I strongly believe that God helps those who help themselves.

Besides, an emergency may also be of the kind that renders you unfit to work. What then? You do not have a partner to depend on. Will you completely rely on your children then? What if you do not have children, or what if they refuse to look after you? How will you live the rest of your life without money then?

I have seen requests to collect donations for old ailing actors in the newspapers. For these actors, who are old, single and ill, without the money to pay for medical treatment, financial help may come one way or the other. But for ordinary people, it's next to impossible.

If you are getting older, and are single, without decent investments to your name, you cannot waste any more time. Earlier, debt instruments were the only choice. As for equity investments, there was only the stock market, which was very risky. But the system has evolved over the past couple of decades. It is now more transparent, with low-risk products you can invest in. If you have a reasonable amount of money, invest right away. You can even put your money in equities. To protect your investment, you may want to choose equity mutual funds rather than directly going to the bourses.

- If, as a single woman, you are financially self-dependent, everybody around you, including your family and children, will respect you.
- If you are not financially independent, you will live an isolated life, and no one will have much regard for you.

I have always said this to my friends, and here I say it again. Nothing is riskier than human relationships, and depending on them can be the riskiest of dependences. If you should depend, depend on yourself. You will notice that when you stand up on your own, you will have more friends and well-wishers than ever. Your children will respect you, even if they are living with your estranged husband or partner. Besides, with self-reliance comes the power to reject. You will feel like your own boss. You can turn down all the proposals which threaten to destroy your romance with life.

People always argue with me whenever I talk about absolute self-dependence. My catchphrase is 'I hate depending.' Every time someone hears me say this for the first time, they usually retort that you cannot get on in life without depending on the people around you. No matter how much of an independent person you are, you still need people to do things for you. I agree! And I don't expect you to become an incorrigible control freak or an indomitable transformer; that is not what I mean when I refer to 'self-dependence'.

When that tap in your bathroom starts to leak, you will need to call a plumber to fix it. If he is not available, you will have to wait. You can't play plumber and try to do it yourself just because the plumber was not available and you were impatient. At work, even as the boss, you cannot do the work of all the departments for them. You will inevitably be dependent on other people. In such cases, your calibre will be tested by the way you manage your team and get quality work done in a pleasant environment. But coming back to what I mean by 'self-dependence': I am using it strictly in terms of money. Make yourself strong when it comes to money.

This is easier said than done in the case of women. It is tough for women to be financially self-dependent because they are conditioned to be dependent. They are brought up with the mindset that one day they will be married and then their husband will fulfil their financial requirements.

No wonder there are so many jokes and stereotypes about women making men spend on them. Even if women are working, they expect men to pay on dates and also give them expensive presents. But this arrangement has to change.

- Women are socially conditioned to depend on their men for money. Break this convention!

To begin with, prepare your budget and account for the most expensive emergency that you imagine might come up in your life. When everything is said and done, when an emergency actually strikes and you still do not have enough, despite having prepared as best as you could, then wait for a miracle. They say that 'God helps those who help themselves.' If you have done all that that is humanly possible to help yourself, then you will not be left stranded. There is a saying in Punjabi which translates as 'If you have milk at home, you will be offered yoghurt outside. But if you have nothing at home, you will not be offered anything outside either.' This sums it up very well. Here 'outside' means anyone who is not you, including your family and friends.

Imagine, as a mother, asking your son or daughter or children-in-law for money for daily expenses. The very thought of it is embarrassing. You may try to rationalize: 'Why should I feel embarrassed? They are my children. They will give me whatever I ask for.' Of course they will, but you will still feel like you are living a borrowed life. You will feel uncomfortable and insecure; you will constantly feel obliged to repay them for the help they are giving you. Avoid this by being independent…financially independent.

As a single mother, the first lesson you must give your children is that of financial independence. Besides this, single mothers must follow the same steps in handling their children's money issues as discussed in the chapter 'The Mother'.

THE STANDARD-BEARER THEORY—AND SOME THINGS TO REMEMBER

When you are a single woman, you do not have much external support. So you will need to take hold of the reins.

- Be financially prepared for your present as well as your future.
- Work towards absolute financial independence.
- Employment is a must for single women.
- Work out a concrete financial plan and stick to it
- If you are rendered single suddenly due to the demise of your spouse, find a job. If you cannot work, put your partner's pension and other income from returns on investments to proper use.
- If you are rendered single because of divorce, take up a job immediately and put a financial plan in place.
- As a single mother, the first lesson you must give to your children is that of the importance of financial independence.

12

The Professional Woman

There was a time when women stepped out to work only in the face of adversity or to add punch to their matrimonial bio-data. We are living in a different time now. In fact, we have come a long way since women ventured out and made a mark in the professional arena. We are at the next level, where challenges begin in the workplace.

From bagging a job to negotiating a salary or promotion, it's one challenge after another. True, these are not women-specific challenges. Men also face these in their professional lives. But research and my own experience reveal that while the challenges may be the same, the situation is very different for women.

- The famous glass ceiling is reeling under its own weight. But we have a long way to go before it shatters.

THE WOMAN WHO REFUSES TO GROW

I have heard of quite a few heads of companies, most of whom are women, complain that no matter how much they encourage their female employees, some women do not progress beyond a certain level. When they join the company at a junior level, these women show a lot of enthusiasm to grow and learn, and they make a lot of effort to achieve their goals. Then something strange happens and their enthusiasm fizzles out midway. They stop working towards a salary hike, they do not care enough to negotiate the hike they get on appraisal. Some women never even negotiate their pay packages while switching jobs.

I found it strange that almost all women should exhibit this recessive trait, especially when we are celebrating women's liberation. But when I analysed the reasons for this behaviour, I realized that there is nothing strange about it. Women are coming out of the shell, no doubt. But this is just the beginning. We are in a phase of transition. Women are yet to completely break the shackles of old-fashioned beliefs that are imposed upon them. At first, women oppose these beliefs even at the risk of being considered rebels. But as life takes over, they start to believe in them. Bogged down by the pressures of multitasking, women tend to take their 'well-wishers' seriously and accept what they get. This is regressive, and thwarts progress.

- Women refuse to fight their way up as the people around them tell them constantly that their salary is secondary to that of their husbands. Such comments serve as deterrents for women.

Now why people try to impose these philosophies on women is a subject worthy of discussion. Generally, they say these things simply because they are unhappy with women's progress; this kind of unhappiness comes from the insecurity of a ruler whose subjects are outsmarting him. You may call it jealousy if you want. It may also be that they really believe in all this.

I have heard an uncle say during a family gathering, 'Women would do well by staying home and bearing children.' Another uncle doesn't let women in his family drive his compact sedan. If he has to go out, he asks our male cousins to drive him. If no men are available, he cancels his trip or asks for a taxi, even if I or other female cousins are around.

Comments and behaviour like this lead to an erosion of enthusiasm and passion among women. Even insignificant statements made casually leave a strong impact on a woman's psyche.

Since the beginning of my career, I have encountered people who have tried their best to brainwash me into believing that whatever I was doing was wrong. A little while ago, when I was a reporter for a magazine, I ran into one of my uncles at a cousin's wedding in Delhi. As we were chatting about this and that, he asked his wife, my aunt, to take out an envelope from his bag. The next moment he was showing off his son-in-law's salary slip! This was absolutely hilarious. Then he asked me what my salary was. I told him. I was earning well, but it was less than what his son-in-law was earning as an engineer.

My uncle said, 'Oh, that's good! But how does it matter? You will be getting married someday. It's always the husband's salary that matters. Your salary is secondary. I feel women should actually not slog.' This was a shocking statement for me. I was doubly amazed that it came from a relative who had spent so much to educate his two daughters. But later I figured out that, in his mind, all that education was only to get good husbands for his daughters.

This uncle's older daughter, who is married to the engineer son-in-law, holds a diploma in textile designing from a highly-reputed institute. She worked for a couple of years before marriage, but quit once she got married. Even her husband asked her why she needed to work when he was making good money and was able to provide well for the family. My uncle had said the same thing to his wife when she expressed the desire to open a boutique after their marriage.

This same uncle visited Mumbai for a day last year. He met me for a couple of hours at a coffee shop and during that brief meeting essentially had only this to say: 'What's all this business you have started? You must get a job somewhere. Back home they say that only those who are otherwise useless start a business!'

But this did not begin after I set up my company. It started when I started talking about my big dreams. When I was sixteen, I wanted to be a fashion designer. I told my parents I wanted to go to the National Institute of Fashion Technology. NIFT had only one centre at that time, in Delhi. When my relatives in Delhi found out about this, my parents received lots of unwanted input like 'NIFT is not a safe place for girls!' As it turned out, I didn't make it past the entrance test, so I never became a fashion designer anyway.

Later, when I told my relatives that I had got a job as a reporter, my decision was opposed by every one of them. They said journalism was not a career for women. Give me a break!

Amazingly—and thankfully—my parents, who had spent most of their lives in a small town like Jabalpur, had a more open outlook. When I told my mother that I had started a company, she was thrilled. Ever since I can recall, my parents have always been enthusiastic and supportive about my career. Though they would worry occasionally about my marriage prospects, the focus was still on my career. I really appreciate this. Of course, it was the same for my brother, but I want to highlight my parents' support for me, as we are talking about our society's outlook on working women. It's because of my parents' progressive mindset that I have reached where I have.

I remember my father telling me once, when I was in college, 'It is very important for women to be independent in life. We have a dream to see you like that.' He had always regretted that my mother left her job as a middle-schoolteacher in Rohtak when they got married. She could have easily got a job in a good school in Jabalpur, and she would have been a principal by now. But my grandparents objected, and my mother gave in thinking it would be unwise to upset her in-laws right at the beginning of her marriage. Then other responsibilities came up in the shape of children, and her return to teaching kept getting postponed indefinitely. Later, when my brother and I had grown up, she felt awkward about returning to a professional life after such a long gap. So she remained a housewife. This is the story of many women of my mother's age group, and some even today.

Women are surrounded by people who have a mindset like that of my relatives. The omnipresence of such a mentality influences women so much so that they start believing in it themselves.

My family's perennial search for a 'suitable boy' for me is still on. I must admit that there is a lack of seriousness on my part when it comes to my own marriage. It's largely because I have a feeling that no matter how open-minded a man is, a woman's ambitions are suppressed to some extent once she ties the knot.

I agree husbands and their relatives are a lot more flexible these days about professional wives and daughters-in-law. As my beautician in Delhi says, 'Husbands know that wives need the same amount of cooling from air conditioners as they do. They know that wives need the same amount of entertainment from the TV as husbands do. This leads to bloated bills, which they can't pay with only one salary. The wife's salary is necessary. So, it's better to respect your working wife and be at peace with her.'

Another reason why I want to put off getting married is that I do not want my children to grow up with nannies while I am busy with work. If I attend to my company, my children will be neglected, and vice versa. My company needs my absolute attention right now. If I get married, I will have to sacrifice one thing for the other. I certainly do not expect my husband to babysit. Right now, as I devote all my time to building my company, it's my own personal life that's is being sacrificed, which does not affect anyone but me.

Wait! How can I say it does not affect anyone? Apparently, it does! It affects my numerous relatives, random neighbours and their relatives, and relatives of relatives whom I have never met and never will. All these people will suggest prospective husbands for you and will burn the midnight oil to try to understand why you aren't married yet. People have mastered the art of baseless judgement.

A family friend dropped in one evening when I was in Delhi in December 2011. He shared my family's concerns about not having found the right match for me yet. I was out for a meeting, and returned that evening after he had left. My mother told me that he was of the opinion that my profession as a journalist, combined with an entrepreneur, overwhelms prospective bridegroom's families. He explained that middle-class families are generally wary of women journalists and if you add entrepreneurship to the mix, it's a deadly combo. Secondly, he said, my resume should be toned down a bit as it exuded high ambition—our society is not yet evolved enough for people to accept daughters-in-law or wives who are already showing signs of professionally overtaking their husbands. The family friend concluded that my family should not reveal my profession to a prospective groom's family during the first conversation they have, and that instead I should tell the prospective groom when I talked to him or met him.

This really shocked me. I was always proud of being an entrepreneur and a scribe. And now here was someone telling me that these were unacceptable professions! I was shocked not because our family friend thought so, but because he was only telling us how society thinks. He is quite social and, being a sales and marketing professional, he has the opportunity to visit various places and meet people from different cultures and social strata. So he was conveying a common perception in society to us. This is how people think. Isn't it enough to discourage a woman? No wonder so many women lose their drive halfway through their working life.

- Men and their families find it hard to accept as wife and daughter-in-law a woman who is professionally ahead of her prospective groom.

There may be a problem if the wife holds a higher designation than her husband, if she is more influential than him, if she earns more than him, and even if she helps him get a better job or a better position. In a nutshell, there will be a problem if the wife is professionally better than her husband in any way. And this applies to brothers too.

I met an entrepreneur at a conference in Mumbai, and we soon became very good friends. One day, about a year after we had met, she went to visit her brother in Delhi. A couple of days later she called me, crying, and told me that her struggling engineer brother had said, 'She thinks she's too smart...yeah, yeah, why not? After all, she is a businesswoman. She is a big shot. She is rich and she thinks I am a big nothing. What is she so snooty about? Her business is not making any profits. Tell her to leave my house. She cannot stay here. Get out!'

He said this in the presence of their mother and two of his friends. She told me that this was not the first time he had said something like this either. He would talk like this whenever he was angry. Even when he wasn't angry, he would insinuate things. He had been doing this ever since she started working and he was rusticated from college because of misconduct. Okay, okay, he was frustrated. But his sister had also faced setbacks in her career, and she was not born successful. Men are always made to understand that they are the stronger sex. And human psychology is such that you attack people who are worse-equipped than you are.

In India, we have a festival called Rakshabandhan. On this day, the sister ties a bracelet on her brother's wrist, and the brother vows to protect her throughout her life. This is regardless of whether the brother is older or younger than the sister, and regardless of who is currently supporting whom.

- Men are fed exaggerated notions about their superiority right from childhood.

I was returning late one night from a family friend's house in Delhi in 2012. Although my home was a two-minute walk away, within the same compound, the family friend insisted that her eleven-year-old son escort me! If there were hooligans waiting to attack me or abduct me, how would an adolescent protect me? I'd rather that they had sent their teenage daughter along with me. Together we would have been a force to reckon with. But, no, the logic is that the very sight of a man in tow will scare away the bad guys.

I must share with you an incident which just struck me. Sometime in 2005, when I was reporting for a news channel, I went to cover an outbreak of dengue deaths and government negligence in a slum in Bandra. The doctors and other hospital staff were operating from a section of a mosque near the slum settlement. I entered the mosque along with our cameraman; while he took some shots in the mosque courtyard, I went to the section where the doctors were. A little later, I heard some chaos outside. I ran out and saw that a mob had gathered in the courtyard. Right in the centre was a camera held up above the mob by a hand. I almost freaked out. I made my way through the angry crowd and reached the cameraman. He was almost in tears! As soon as he saw me, he cried out, 'Shruti, please take me out of here.'

Surprised at his reaction, I turned to the old men who were surrounding us. They said it was against their religion to photograph or shoot corpses. They wouldn't let the cameraman go without deleting the video he had been taking. I turned to him and told him to delete the video. He said he had not been filming the bodies, so I told him to show the footage to the old men as proof. He said he would, but first I needed to get him out of there. I assured the men that nothing had been shot, and that they had my word that if there was a video, we would not use it. I 'rescued' my cameraman and escorted him to the car. After that, I had originally planned to take a tour of the slum and shoot some footage. But my cameraman refused to get out of the car! So I had to take the camera and shoot everything myself that day. This cameraman must be the brother of some sister whom he would have vowed to protect.

I never told anyone at work about this incident. Some of my friends and acquaintances know about the incident, but not who the cameraman was; I will never reveal his identity because it would subject him to tremendous embarrassment. People would not even shy away from calling him a sissy for behaving as he did. You see, men are not supposed to weep in public. It implies that they are weak. There are a lot of 'feminine' things men are not supposed to do.

My father was very fond of pakoras, and since Jabalpur is blessed with a long rainy season, pakoras enjoyed a special place at the top of the daily menu for a good part of the year. My father loved experimenting when it came to pakoras, and our huge kitchen garden helped. From chopping vegetables to dredging them in besan and frying them, he did it all. When my relatives in Delhi found out about this, they made fun of him. One morning one of my uncles called to speak to my father, and I answered. My father was on the lawn, reading the newspaper. I asked my uncle to hold the line while I fetched my father. He immediately joked, 'Is he in the kitchen?'

My brother is also very fond of cooking. Last year, when my mother went to visit him in Delhi, she decided to cook mushrooms one day. A friend of my brother's, who had come to see him, told him, 'This smells really good. Learn how to cook this, so that you can make it for us when auntie leaves.

If men do certain things, they will be regarded as weak and effeminate, and be mocked every now and then. When they beat or shout at women at home, it gives them an exaggerated sense of their masculinity, which has been inculcated in them ever their since childhood by their families (including their mothers, grandmothers, aunts, etc.).

This is the same society which is now telling women that their salary is secondary to their men's. Earlier there was no need to make women cognisant of their 'subordinate' status, because almost all women accepted what came their way. But now, things are different. Many women of this generation have seen their mothers live a restricted life, and now they refuse to accept the age-old status quo. This is what has led to problems in families. But, like I said, it's women who can bring about change, and sustain it as well. Society will have to accept it at some point.

- Women will have to play change-makers by reaching over the limits set by age-old worn-out beliefs. Society is too weak to stand up to change, and it's too selfish to unite towards causing change.

If you have worked hard to achieve success, you should not give up so easily. Strive and grow in your professional capacity. Women, who get bogged down by the age-old diktats forced upon them by their 'well-wishers' ruin their careers and their personal lives as well. Later, they regret their 'number two' status and their decision to give up their careers or not work hard enough to grow.

So, wake up now. Your salary is not secondary to anyone else's. You slog as much as your male colleagues in office. In fact, you work twice as hard if you also run your household. The woman in a family is the first to wake up in the morning and the last to hit the sack in the night. You must not underestimate your profession or your calibre.

- Turn a deaf ear to words like 'A woman's salary is only supplementary to her husband's.'

As it is, the glass ceiling that we hear about is intact. Women get paid less than their male counterparts, and they lag behind men when it comes to salaries and financial decision-making at home, even if it is the woman's money being invested. So exert yourself, and get what is rightfully yours. We may see the glass ceiling crumbling sometime soon. Do not let your head get filled with the rotten stuff that your numerous 'well-wishers' feed you.

Another reason for women not fighting it out for higher salaries and designations is because with a fatter pay packet come bigger expectations and responsibilities at work. Since women have to multitask, handling both office and household responsibilities at the same time, they prefer to continue being low-key in office. They refrain from taking up larger responsibilities that will require more from them. They prefer to compromise in their professional life rather than personal life, because at home they run the risk of interrupting the peace of the household if they show any reluctance to handle responsibilities.

But I have a solution to this. If you want a higher salary, change jobs; find yourself a position where there are an equal or greater number of responsibilities but more pay. Another solution is to talk to your husband about sharing responsibilities at home. You can divide your responsibilities equally; having your husband handle half the tasks will reduce your burden and help you handle more work in office, opening up opportunities for professional growth. If this arrangement works out between couples, it is a blessing. Usually it's not that easy, because no matter how much we talk about sharing household responsibilities, it's women who end up doing the majority of the household work.

Well, old mindsets die hard. When my mother visited my brother's flat in Delhi for the first time, she pointed out to one of his flatmates that the house and the bathrooms were untidy. The twenty-something pilot had the audacity to reply, 'Auntie, keeping the house and bathrooms clean is a woman's job!' This happened as recently as March 2011. They had a maid but her job was limited to sweeping and mopping. So the bathrooms stayed dirty for a month, and the men would clean them only when they had started literally stinking.

It's not just your parents' or your grandparents' generation. Even today, young men think in old ways. Women will have to multitask unless they are blessed with a very understanding or a very rich husband, who can afford domestic help to manage all the household work without supervision; because if any supervision is required, it will again be the woman's responsibility.

Coming back to promotions and salaries, I must mention one very important aspect which comes into the picture every time a woman is promoted or gets a salary hike. Once, a man I had met during an official assignment in Goa asked me, 'I have heard that there is a lot of sleeping around in journalism, just like in the world of cinema. Is this true? Do women need to do all this to make it big in this field?' This really shocked me! This man had studied and lived in the UK for nine years, and this was his mentality! He continued, 'I'm just asking because I have never met a journalist before, and I have heard all these stories about this profession.' This cheesed me off. But I kept my calm and answered, 'I won't be of much help here. You might want to "interview" some other journalists about this. Shall I forward you some contact details?' When women are doing well in their careers, people usually take it with a pinch of salt.

It's very sad, and also irritating, that people connect women's professional growth with illicit relationships. There may be some cases where women use their femininity to get ahead, but if that happens, it comes to light soon enough, because her progress lasts only as long as the relationship. If a woman has ability, she will make it through rough terrain on her own without her sexuality. If she relies only on sexual favours, she won't go very far.

You may get a raise or two with these methods. But at the end of the day, it's your work that matters. Imagine that you have no talent and no knowledge of the work you have to do and you use your sexuality to climb professionally. Sometime later, you have a junior working for you who is really good at her work. She will soon discover your true calibre. She will not be able to respect you. She will hate you. It will be difficult to work together. If this happens several times, the axe may fall on you. You will be left with a filthy feeling of, 'I sold my soul for this?!'

I had a roommate who would frequently crib about her (female) boss's low efficiency. I thought this was just the usual boss-bashing. But one day my friend took me along to an office party at the company's owner's home. I saw my roommate's boss mingling with the owner of the company. As they got drunk they got physically closer and closer. By midnight, they had disappeared, even as the owner's wife looked on. A couple of days later, my roommate's boss was sacked.

Easy routes never take you to the right destination. Take the longer, tougher routes. Strive. Even if you do not reach your destination, you will not end up bruised halfway down the road.

Okay, now that you are all set to strike a deal, let me tell you that all this career growth and all these inflated pay packages will be useless if you do not manage your salaries intelligently. For the first two years of your working life, you can splurge and have fun to your heart's content. After that, get serious. Start budgeting, and follow your budget religiously. This may not be easy because our society has moulded women to be dependants. Like all human beings, women also enjoy being dependent until they realize that they are compromising their freedom.

So start getting involved in managing your salary while you are still unmarried. If you do so, your fiancé will know from the start that you are independent enough, and he will automatically leave your finances to you even after you are married.

- Start budgeting and planning your finances a couple of years after you start your first job.

Spend an hour or two every weekend learning about personal finance and updating yourself about your investments and cash flow. Do this even if the male members of your family are investing your money for you. If you are already married and have not thought of this yet, it's not too late. Start now!

I am sure you do not want to be embarrassed like this woman I met during an assignment. The personal finance magazine I worked for had decided to feature a profile of a woman who had invested about seven lakhs in the stock market. I spoke to her on the phone before visiting her, and when I arrived at her home, we began talking about her career. When I moved on to her investments, I started by asking her, 'You are heavily invested in equities. What do you think about the markets as they are now?' She replied, 'Shruti, I'm sorry, but I don't know anything about that. I do not understand equities at all. In fact, I don't know what equities are. Can we please continue this interview after my husband arrives?' That was really shocking. I would never have expected this from a high-ranking official with a market research company. To top it all, she had a huge chunk of her salary invested in shares. Well, obviously, the profile was never published in the magazine.

The moral of this story is not that women should not let their husbands invest their money on their behalf. But as a professional woman, you are expected to be actively involved in the proceedings. Most working women are adequately educated and are aware of what goes on around them, and they handle crucial responsibilities at the office. But strangely, when it comes to personal finance management, which is simpler than the balance sheets they manage at work, they prefer to leave it to the male members of their families. That's a bad move. Be actively involved in the management of your finances. And even if your husband owns a house, buy another in your name. In your old age, if your children plan to send you to a home for the elderly, you can dodge them and stay in the house you own yourself.

When I started my company, I happened to meet a family in Mumbai; I saw their six-year-old daughter performing at a function and decided to invite them for a stage conversation for my company's very first money management event for women and children. We have kept in touch ever since. About a year ago, the little girl's mother, an interior designer, called to tell me that she had bought a flat, since the flat they live in right now is registered under her husband's name. This was definitely a move in the right direction.

- As a working woman, make sure that you know what is happening to your money.

Coming back to what I said above, I must advise you that while you fight for salary hikes and plan your spending and saving, make sure that you are doing enough to keep your job. After a certain point, you may not be very welcome in your own family if you do not have an income.

In case you are married and lose your job for some reason, you will not feel very good about asking your husband to fund your future. You may feel embarrassed, as if you have to keep your back bent a bit as you move on with life. It may seem that you have all the liberties that anybody could ask for, but actually your freedom will be curbed to a large extent. So measure your steps when treading the professional line. It's a tightrope.

- After you get married, don't be in a hurry to stop working. Keep your job, no matter what. For women who have lived a professional, financially independent life, it's usually difficult to accept an arrangement where they have to function under the vigilance of men.

There may also be problems if you are unmarried, and, having lost your job, move in with your family, where your brother (whether younger or older) also lives. Mark my words: it's all about money.

One of my friends resigned from her lucrative job in a huff. After a few months, she couldn't find another job, and her savings were dwindling steadily, so she decided to give up her rented flat in Mumbai and move to her brother's home in Delhi. Their mother was also living there at the time. One day, one of her brother's friends came over. My friend was sitting in the balcony talking to one of her ex-colleagues, and she happened to use the F-word. The brother went into the kitchen to get a snack; meanwhile, his friend started eavesdropping on my friend's phone conversation. When my friend's brother came back from the kitchen, the first thing his friend did was to inform him that his elder sister had used the F-word, and that this was not right when their mother was around. The brother had checked his friends' profanity several times, and the friend was taking the opportunity to bring to his attention that his own sister used profanities, so how could he correct them.

My friend's brother immediately got up, barged into the balcony and shouted at his sister. The sister, who was still on the phone, was startled. Then she hung up the phone and said, 'I know my limits. You need not shout.' This made the brother furious. He got louder. His friend sat there enjoying his snack. The brother then attacked his sister physically, pulling her by her arm and asking her to leave his house. When their mother intervened, he asked her to pack up her stuff and leave along with his sister. My friend ended up with black and blue marks on her arms. The next day the friend came to her to 'apologize', and told her that her brother was just 'short-tempered'.

My friend has had one steady relationship for the last

five years. She has worked at very high positions with reputed companies. She had to leave her last job because the company had not raised their employees' salaries for the last two years, citing the economic crunch as the reason. Though she still had enough savings, she could not afford to maintain her lifestyle in Mumbai on her own. But when you are living in a family, living expenses come down. So, her mother advised her to move in with her brother in Delhi. Like anyone else in her situation, she thought she had her family and brother to fall back on. All of us think that way. But this may not be true if you have a struggling sibling, especially a struggling brother.

In this case too, the reason behind the brother's rage was money—rather, the lack of money. He was out of a job, and he had a loan to repay. Of late, his 'close friends' who had been lending him money and were his companions in all the world's pleasures that came with alcohol, tobacco and women, had had to keep away from his place as his family was present. So, no parties at the flat. What also frustrated him was the thought that now he had responsibilities and no money.

Whatever it was, he could have talked about it, rather than beating up his sister and yelling at his mother. This madness was repeated several times; each time, for a new but equally silly reason. But the mother held the family together by begging the sister not to move out. Finally, the family had to get help from a friend who is a leadership trainer. He started counselling the brother and slowly persuaded him to start thinking more logically. Later, both my friend and her brother got very good jobs, and started living separately. Peace prevailed.

But what is evident from such incidents is that if men are going through a financially difficult patch in their lives, women have to bear the brunt of it. Some men, after beating the women in their lives, tell them, 'Don't worry. I will be the one taking care of you eventually. Soon, I will have a lot of money.' In other words, 'Till then, please do not mind when I beat you up.' Quite some logic!

I think that after a certain age, generally after you cross thirty, if you have to struggle in your career again, it's best to avoid staying with your family, especially if there is a struggling brother around. Even if everything is going well, your struggling brother's 'well-wisher' friends may decide to bless your stay with their holy intervention like in my friend's case.

A lack of money in men's lives causes frustration, which, more often than not, is taken out on women. Actually, traditionally, women are used to getting beaten up and men are used to beating them up. I have been witness to a sixty-year-old woman being shouted at by her son. When she could not take it any more, she shouted back, but the son was much louder and she did not have the strength to shout any louder. So she decided to take the crap silently and pray for her son to calm down. The same goes for sisters and wives. Men are physically stronger than women and when the going gets tough in their lives, they use this strength to take their frustration out on women

But as women are becoming financially more independent,

many women are protesting this suppression. When it becomes unbearable, they just end the relationship or marriage, or walk out of the house.

So, before giving up your job, make sure you have enough saved to sustain you for at least a year, or you have another job in hand. If you are sacked, accept an offer even if they are paying you less than what you were earning. Move to a smaller apartment. Reduce your expenses. Lie low till you get back to your earlier income level.

Do not misunderstand me. I am not trying to distance you from your siblings by telling you not to fall back on them. Rather, I am telling you how to maintain cordiality in the family. In certain situations in life, physical distance helps bring the family closer. Also, I am telling you to refrain from being financially dependent on your struggling siblings. If your unmarried brother is very well-settled, then there should not be a problem with you staying with him. I specified 'unmarried' because after marriage, you may feel uncomfortable about turning up at your brother's place lock, stock and barrel, jobless. It's not just him in the picture; his wife or family may be averse to your moving in.

This applies when you are young and still capable of managing your unemployed status. But as you age and move closer to retirement, you will be completely dependent on the people around you, and more often than not, they will be your children. But as I have described, we are fast moving towards a nuclear family system, where even parents are not staying with their children. Take your cue from the number of senior citizens living alone or with their spouses.

Recently, I met two men on different occasions, who both told me, 'I don't want my mother to come and live with me. It gets too "mom", you see. There's a question about every move you make. It's better to live separately, so that both of you can enjoy your freedom.' One of these men is a Bollywood actor, the other is a mechanical engineer in Mumbai. The actor lives in Santa Cruz and his mother lives on Peddar Road, a good forty-minute drive away. The engineer's mother lives in Bangalore. Both the mothers are working widows.

Most sons and even unmarried daughters prefer not to live with their parents. Seeing this, I strongly feel that working women should have a retirement corpus in place. Children are no guarantee for old age.

If you have plans to retire, start building a retirement corpus as early as possible. I say 'if' because these days many people plan to keep working even after the official retirement age. Even if you are one of these people, I still suggest you have a retirement corpus ready. I know a lot of old women whose children were not really settled until after their mother's retirement, but were still financially dependent on their mothers, who lived on their late husbands' pensions and their own savings.

- A retirement corpus is a must for single women. They should start working towards it as early as possible.

It would not be wise to just assume that your children will take care of your financial requirements after you retire. What if your daughters-in-law or your sons-in-law or even your own children turn out to be callous towards the feelings of their old mother? Even if they are not thankless or uncaring, they may prefer to live their lives separately from you. Old age homes are teeming with women who have been abandoned by their own children. But if you have a retirement corpus in place, you will be fine on your own.

THE PRO STRATAGEM THEORY—AND SOME THINGS TO REMEMBER

As a professional woman, you must have a strategy which is definitely very different from that of a professional man.

- Fight for a salary hike. The world will tell you that your salary is only secondary to your husband's. Turn a deaf ear to this. Work towards your own professional growth.
- As a married working woman, do not consider your salary mere pocket money. Plan to use some part of your salary along with your husband's for family expenses.
- Budget your salary. After earmarking a part of your salary for family expenses, allocate the rest for investments, etc. Take personal financial planning very seriously.
- Single working women should start financial planning very early in life. Plan your finances in the first ten years of your career.

- Do not take the easy route. Do not sleep around for money or for professional growth.
- Stay in your present job till you get another one. Stay if you do not have enough money to sustain yourself for at least a year after quitting.
- If you are suddenly unemployed, it's not a good idea to move in with a struggling sibling.
- Plan your retirement. Start building a retirement corpus as early as possible.
- Own a house. Buy property.

13

The Entrepreneur

Entrepreneurs are a different subject altogether. And for women entrepreneurs, it's a whole other ballgame. Entrepreneurial issues, whether for whether men or women, revolve around funds, profits, and scaling, and there is the need to tread with caution.

When referring to women entrepreneurs, I can start by talking about my own experience. Being a first-generation entrepreneur, I faced many money-related situations, several of which I hadn't expected, given all my years of experience in the workplace. To begin on a mild note, people usually want to know how my venture is being funded. Of course, there is nothing objectionable about this. But being asked the same question umpteen times when you have already told them umpteen times that it is self-funded? It's the way it is asked that annoys me.

If you are married, people assume your venture is being funded by your husband. But if you are single and start a venture, they will get 'bright' ideas about the source of your funds. In such situations, don't get outraged, or raise your voice. There's no need to come across as aggressive right at the beginning of your new journey. However, there's no need to be too nice either. Be sarcastic but polite. And try to ignore such queries as much as you can.

Of course, funding is the most important aspect of your business, second only to your business idea. So, once you have done your research and finalized the idea, work out the funds. They can come from various sources. In businesses like franchises and distribution of established brands or other businesses, where you are sure about immediate profits, you can source your initial capital through loans. For other businesses, where it's investments first and profits later, the initial capital should come from your pocket. That's the safest and the best way for women entrepreneurs, especially single women. That's how I did it.

The idea for my venture occurred to me as early as 2003. But I wanted to get some firsthand experience in the media and also be sure about the focus of my publications. At that time I could only see mainstream news magazines and newspapers doing good business. In 2004, I left my job as a newspaper reporter to devote some time to aggressive research on entrepreneurship. However, I could not be unemployed in the meanwhile. So I joined a start-up magazine which would provide an income, give me the time to continue my research, and also give me an opportunity to gain firsthand knowledge about how start-ups work.

It was a business-to-business magazine. It had six

employees when I joined; I was the seventh. Incidentally, even though I was unemployed when I approached them, I was offered a salary that was twenty-five per cent more than my previous pay package. That was my first lesson in entrepreneurship. Even though you run a small company, you will attract talent if you are a good paymaster.

This was a turning point for me for another reason as well. My stint at the magazine opened me up to the idea of niche media. I started exploring this field, and a couple of months later, I quit to spend more of my time researching, along with hunting for a job in news channels.

Over the next three years, I worked with both an English and a Hindi news channel. Around this time, I decided that the focus of my company would be personal finance. Since I was a science graduate with no background in finance, I decided to report for a personal finance magazine to gain a foundation in finance. I chose a magazine over a newspaper or channel, because it gave me ample time after office hours to plan my venture. By the end of 2009, I had floated my company. It's been more than three years now and I have enough savings to fund the venture for another year.

I never used any outlandish tactics to work out my budget for my business. But yes, I admit, it did require extra effort from me. Journalism, especially print journalism where I spent most of my professional life, is not a very well-paid profession, compared with IT and sales and marketing. So, I had to work extra-hard to be able to save enough money in the next six years. Between 2003 and 2009, I lived in accommodation where the rent was fairly low. I hardly went out with my friends; I was never a party person, and as a teetotaller and a non-smoker, I saved on these expenses too. My expenditure was chiefly on the basic essentials of life and, yes, on books. But that was also very economically managed.

A lot of saving went into my initial capital. But it was not very difficult for me to follow these ways of saving money. In fact, it came almost naturally to me: I learnt it from my parents. As a government official, my father did not earn a lot, even though the perks of the job were impressive.

My parents taught me that no matter what your salary is, you can become rich by managing your money intelligently while you are still young enough to slog it out. I did exactly that during my initial professional years.

My father was strictly against taking bribes. He had the reputation of being such an honest officer that even the bosses to whom he did not report directly asked for his opinion while drawing up major projects. His honesty and simplicity were the talk of the town. As a result, my brother and I are deeply against bribery. We refused to pay a single penny whenever we had to go to a government office to sort out my father's pension and for any other paperwork. Amazingly, they always asked us for money. As a consequence, our paperwork was delayed for over seven years because without being bribed the officials concerned sat tight like jammed machines and on the other hand, we would not budge to supply them their 'grease'.

All my parents' material possessions came from what they saved from my father's salary. It took him some time to build up his assets, but he did it all with his savings. My mother also never had any really large expenses. Once, when I was talking to my friend Jacqueline, we both wondered how our parents had managed to have a house and several other assets with their humble salaries. We earn triple or quadruple what they earned, and neither of us can even dream owning a decent flat without a loan. The conclusion we arrived at was that our parents had little or no leisure expenses, whereas each time we went out on weekends we coughed up at least five to eight per cent of our salaries. This is minus a shopping spree every now and then. We have more opportunities to spend these days, and saving is regarded as something old-fashioned by our generation.

While planning the budget for my business, I kept all these things in mind. There was no 'extra' expense. For three months after leaving my job at *India Today*, I operated out of a Barista outlet, which was right below my flat. Then I found a shared office space a stone's throw away from my house in Bandra. My travel expenses were nil, and since it was a shared office, the rent was very low. A few months later, I found an independent flat, again near my house, which came cheap as it was in an old building. But it was spacious enough for my team, so I went ahead and shifted my office there.

I always wanted my venture to be self-funded. My plan was that once it was a little more settled and had started making a constant income, even if not a profit, then I would think about external funding if I needed to. But I was strictly against borrowing the initial capital.

Even while borrowing, I have some restrictions. If I ever borrow any money, it will only be in the form of a loan from a bank. I will avoid individual investors, unless it is through a very professional process or the investor is someone whom I know.

Do not be surprised when your male acquaintances who 'admire your guts' offer to invest in your venture, and, when you ask them about the repayment arrangement, revert with, 'You can pay in kind.' They may even want to be partners in your venture. As a single woman, you have to beware these partners who want to be repaid in 'kind'. Even if they offer to get financial help for you from their friends or associates, just to make it look indirect, you must refuse.

The best solution in such situations is to let it go. Do not fall for the bait. Your company's reputation and honour are at stake, along with your own.

Another clause that I added to my book of rules for women entrepreneurs relates to 'business dinners' with individuals. It is fine if you are going out with someone you know or feel comfortable with, otherwise I see no point in these dinners. Lunch is no less productive. Try it. You may think and talk better while the sun is shining. Personally, I have always refused one-on-one business dinners. My business has flourished by way of professional meetings over lunch, brunch and early evening coffee.

The other aspect of these dinners is getting dropped back home after the meal. The offer of a ride invariably comes with the invitation to dinner. Make your own arrangements, please. It's not that you will always be forced into an illicit relationship on the drive home. But it's also a matter of dignity. This will go down as a favour. Women entrepreneurs and even professionals have to refuse any kind of favour, even if it costs them the deal. Your dignity is more important than some frivolous deal.

I must tell you about a 'business dinner' due to which I lost a lucrative deal. My company's revenue model is similar to that of any media company: we make money through advertisements on our website and through sponsorship of our events. When I launched my company in 2009, I approached several relevant companies for advertisements. A couple of reputed companies signed quarterly and half-yearly contracts with us; even though these were at very low rates, it was still a good beginning. These contracts were signed in the first two months after our launch, but we were still searching for more advertisements.

One day I got a call from the executive chairman of a financial services company whom I had met while I was still a reporter. He congratulated me on my new venture and we discussed it in detail. In the course of our conversation, he asked me about the revenue model. When I mentioned advertisements, he immediately said that he would put in a word at his office, and that the next morning I would get a call from their marketing division. I did. They offered me a very good deal! I thought all my efforts were finally paying off. Things were moving really fast; I got the first phone call from the head of marketing on Tuesday. We were supposed to sign the contract on the following Monday.

On Friday afternoon that week, the marketing team

confirmed that things were on track. A little later that day, the executive chairman called. I told him about the contract. Then he asked me if I was free for dinner that evening. Since business dinners do not exist for me, I told him I was expecting guests who were staying the weekend with me.

I never got that call from the marketing team of the company on Monday. I called them on Wednesday and the head of marketing said, 'Shruti, our top bosses are here. We will be busy with them for a week.' The following weekend I received another call from their executive chairman. He wanted to treat me to dinner at the Taj Mahal Palace hotel. I had an excuse once again and I turned down the offer, though this time I did ask him if he was free for lunch. He said he was not. The following week I called their head of marketing again. He said the company was working out its budgets, and nothing could be done for the next six months now. The massive deal had disappeared before it even materialized. But I never regretted it.

I made some very stringent rules for myself when I started my career. Later, when I started my business, these rules became even stricter. I promised myself right at the beginning of my career that I would never trade my character for success. So far I have managed to stick to my diktats, and I trust myself to do so for the rest of my life. I may not be a great leader for the world yet, but for my team I am a leader, all right. I have to set an example for them and they will find it easier to work with me if they can respect me.

As a single woman on your way to lead, set standards for yourself and stick to them. Remember, your company's reputation depends on you. Your company is your baby, whom you are carrying in your arms while you tread all that rough terrain. You falter, your baby falls. You stumble, your company collapses. Mind your step!

Women have to be more careful, because a man can easily pass off as a 'womanizer', which is now an acceptable term to use. Men who are smitten by your looks and achievements will naturally want to get a piece of you. Send them packing. And I am mentioning all this here in this book about money, because most of these pleasures either lead to unnecessary erosion of funds along with your reputation, or these things are done to make easy money for the business.

In a bid to make quick money, you may do something which you regret later. So, be careful and take the tough route. Rather than giving in to the idea of easy money, spend your time finding new ways to make your venture earn money.

This also applies to married women who are running their husband's business, but have suddenly realized their hidden ambition, and are now fighting to come out of their husbands' shadow. They want to be seen as independent entrepreneurs. They are uneasy about their husbands funding the company they run. In hurriedly following such recently-unleashed ambition, they may be lured by easy money. And for them, this is bound to do double damage. While it dents their reputation, it also damages their personal lives, in all probability ruining their marriages in the long run.

If you are running your husband's or your in-laws' business, it's best to play figurehead. If you can, add value with your ideas, and do all you can to help the company grow. If you have discovered some hidden talents within yourself, put them to work to take the company to new heights. You will get your due share of credit before you realize it. Nature's law is very fair in its judgement: every person is rewarded according to their contribution or actions. So, rather than wasting time announcing to the world how splendid you are, set your goals and work towards them, even as your husband takes care of the funds.

If you were running a business on your own before your marriage and you are continuing to run it, you must be in full control. You must also stick to what I suggested for single women. If your husband wants to invest in your venture, wait for a few years after your marriage before you let him. Some women who have just got married may not like my advice. But you have to figure out all the possibilities before you take a decision which will directly or indirectly influence the future of your baby. Remember, it's the proportion of money that decides the proportion of power. The person who has more money commands more influence.

Get to know your husband and his family better, and let them know you too, before officially letting them into your business. You never know what people are thinking. They may have some plans for your venture which you may not approve of. If you give them a big stake in your company without knowing their plans, you will not be in a position to reject their suggestions. They will be empowered to impose their ideas on you, both emotionally and legally.

I have a friend who started a handicrafts business. Her

products became a rage in the area she lived. She started planning to expand her business. Meanwhile, she got married to someone whom she had been seeing for about five years. Before their marriage, he had only shown a casual interest in her company. Three months after their marriage, he suddenly wanted to quit his job and 'do something of his own'. The closest and the softest target was his wife's business. She agreed because 'he's my husband…he's family!'

About six months later, he 'had a great idea'. He suggested that they sell the business. They would immediately get a lot of money, which they could use to start another more lucrative business. My friend was taken aback. She asked him what business he was planning to start. He said he was not sure yet. She suggested that they first plan the next business, and then think about selling the existing one. But her husband was adamant about selling it right then so as to make a quick buck. Thus was a domestic war sparked off. Sometime during that war, I met my friend. She had a scar on her forehead and right cheek. She was now applying for a divorce. The business suffered. The marriage suffered.

However, it's not always bad. I know another instance where the business did very well when a couple worked on it together. But there was one big difference here from the example above. The husband started taking an active interest in his wife's venture only after three years of their being married. Both the partners had known each other for a long time before their marriage; they had been dating for eight years, but had never interfered much in each other's professional lives. Also, the husband did not leave his job and hijack his wife's business.

Four years after their marriage, when the husband started getting involved in his wife's business, he did not become an official partner in the business. He only got involved to the extent of proposing ideas to expand the business. He never funded the company. The wife was in full control of the company budget. Her salary was divided between her own account and the joint account that she had with her husband. This is impressive, and should be a model for other couples in similar situations. Think and plan before you take big decisions which can affect your personal and professional life.

As for handling financial responsibilities after marriage, the same system that I outlined for working women applies to women entrepreneurs. In addition, you must make sure that people do not look at your business as your hobby. They must not think it's some sort of home-grown vegetable which can be taken for granted. You have to make it clear to them that it's even more serious than a regular job. But as an entrepreneur you have added responsibilities, and they will have to excuse you from socializing too much, which you can afford when you are in a regular job.

THE PERCEPTUAL SUPERIORITY THEORY—AND SOME THINGS TO REMEMBER

Understand your position of superiority and let the world understand it too. But impose your authority rationally on yourself as well as the people concerned. Your position of power should not go to your head and make you do things which may be harmful for your company's reputation.

- Strictly avoid easy money. This type of money can be earned only through means which will harm your reputation, as well as your company's.
- If you are a single woman, and people frequently question the source of your money, ignore such queries. If you want to react, be sarcastic but polite. Do not get loud under any circumstances.
- The initial capital should come from your own money. Let your venture be self-funded for as long as possible. Work out a business plan which will ensure that profits start flowing in much before you require outside funding for your venture.
- If you are running your husband's business, it's best to play figurehead. If you have some untapped talents or qualities of leadership in the course of it, apply them under the aegis of your husband or in-laws. If you make a sincere effort, it will be noticed.
- If you have your own business before marriage, make sure you know your husband and in-laws very well before letting them invest their in your venture. It's the proportion of money that decides the proportion of power.

Parting Words

If you are reading this, chances are you have read the whole book. In that case, I hope you have found what you were looking for from this book.

As I have said already, at different stages of our lives, we behave differently. We behave differently in different relationships too. The stakes, for a woman, are forever high when it comes to money. She has to be politically, apolitically, technically, emotionally and in every worldly and otherworldly way be just right when talking about or dealing with money. She falters a bit, and the first and the strongest attack is on her character. She will have to live with labels such as 'loose' or 'incompetent' throughout her life.

If a bride's parents can't load her with enough goodies, she might end up being harassed. If a woman depends on her husband for money, she will have to take his whims and tantrums lying down. If an unmarried woman depends on her siblings, she will not be respected. If a woman's ambition is to be rich, she is considered immoral.

At a New Year's Eve party at a friend's apartment in Delhi, a female friend said her ambition was to see a crore as her salary per month from September 2013 onwards. A male friend responded: 'You are so after money! Look at what happens to women who are greedy for money. More often than not, they end up in bed with the wrong people.'

If a woman is rising in her career, the credit goes to her smart use of femininity. An ambitious woman is usually seen as 'available'—it is assumed that she will do anything to be successful.

In October 2012, I was invited for an interview by a well-known FM channel in Delhi. While recording the conversation, the RJ said 'women and money' while introducing my magazine. He immediately stopped, switched off the recording and said, 'We need another phrase. "Women and money" together sounds sort of...I guess, cheap.'

These mindsets need to change. Financial independence should lead to true independence for women, and for that, attitudes and behaviours have to evolve—I hope that this book contributes in some small way to that change.

I hope this book will help at least some of its readers reorganize their relationship with money, vis a vis other relationships, and also retune their outlook towards financial independence of other women.

I also hope that some men will have taken out time to read this book and remember the lessons herein—because, like they say, it takes two to tango!

Acknowledgements

When Rupa approached me in October 2011 with a proposal to write a book on women and money, I thought I had met enough people and had enough stories to do so. I had been editing my company's magazine on financial independence for women (it was restructured to provide a broader platform to include all sorts of independence for women and renamed *The Petticoat Journal* in November 2012). But I was wrong.

I was yet to meet an ex-colleague from a media organization, who was to tell me about his colleague who turned up in office with a bruised forehead and jaw one morning. The previous night, she had been watching a show on TV when her mother-in-law asked her for a cup of tea; she'd responded saying that she'd make it in two minutes, when the show broke for commercials. Hearing this, her father-in-law had hit her with a golf club even as her husband looked on. Her father-in-law is a retired bureaucrat, her husband is a serving bureaucrat, her mother-in-law is a professor, she is a journalist.

I was yet to meet nineteen-year-old Bhumika, an engineering student who belongs to a village in Loni in Ghaziabad. She was a devoted protestor at the demonstrations after the Delhi gang rape incident of 16 December 2012. She was proud that in her village women are very safe. 'Look at me. I am wearing jeans and a T-shirt. But no one has ever passed a lewd comment in my village,' she said. According to her, in her village there was zero sexual harassment. She went on to say that in Delhi such instances were so common because 'Delhi girls are too open and unusually modern and that's because they are financially independent.' However, in the case of the gang rape against which she was protesting, she strongly felt that it was not the victim's fault.

I was yet to meet Imarti Devi of Hirmathala village near Delhi. Three years back, when a non-profit organization was providing toilets in her village, she felt her family needed one desperately. But being a daily wage labourer with an unemployed husband and four children, she did not have the money to pay the cost (Rs 3,000) upfront. The organization offered to lend her the money, which she could repay in instalments. But she refused. Instead, she offered to work as a labourer in the construction of the toilets in her village. Her salary of three months served as the payment for the toilet at her house. She told me, 'Why live with debt when I could do something pay it off now?'

I thank my ex-colleague, Bhumika, and Imarti Devi for sharing their thoughts and experiences with me. Their thoughts, lives and circumstances have informed the opinions and suggestions I have put forward in this book.

I also thank all the families and men and women who narrated their stories and allowed me to publish them in this book. One lady said to me, 'If my unpleasant experiences can serve as a lesson for someone else and save them from trauma, I would have served humanity.'

This book owes everything to the cooperation of the wonderful people I met during the course of writing it; to the encouragement and support of my little family; to the inspiration and reassurance of my English teacher in school, Ms Jenny Vyse; and to the motivation and wise counsel provided by my best friend, Sanjeev Choudhary.

Last but the not the least, I thank Pradipta Sarkar, commissioning editor at Rupa Publications India, for providing me with diversions from many ups and downs.

Thank you, all, and be around! Your love and support will never be enough.

www.ingramcontent.com/pod-product-compliance
Lightning Source LLC
Chambersburg PA
CBHW020354170426
43200CB00005B/163